Communicating on

InfoTech

Series Editor: Sue Hewer

7

Communicating on-line

Sabine Gläsmann

The views expressed in this publication are the author's and do not necessarily represent those of CILT.

Acknowledgements

The author would like to thank Claire Dugard for her continued support and recommendations throughout the work on this manuscript.

In some cases it has not been possible to trace copyright holders of material reproduced in this book. The publisher will be pleased to make the appropriate arrangement with any copyright holder whom it has not been possible to contact at the earliest opportunity.

First published 2004 by CILT, the National Centre for Languages 20 Bedfordbury, London WC2N 4LB

Copyright © CILT 2004

ISBN 1 904243 13 4

A catalogue record for this book is available from the British Library

All rights reserved. No part of this publication may be reproduced, stored in a retrieval system, or transmitted by any other means, electronic, mechanical, photocopying, recording or otherwise without prior permission in writing from CILT or under licence from the Copyright Licensing Agency Limited, of 90 Tottenham Court Road, London W1T 4LP.

Sabine Gläsmann has asserted her right to be identified as author of this work, in accordance with the Copyright, Designs and Patents Act, 1988.

Printed in Great Britain by Hobbs

CILT Publications are available from: **Central Books**, 99 Wallis Rd, London E9 5LN. Tel: 0845 458 9910. Fax: 0845 458 9912. Book trade representation (UK and Ireland): **Broadcast Book Services**, Charter House, 29a London Rd, Croydon CR0 2RE. Tel: 020 8681 8949. Fax: 020 8688 0615.

Contents

1	Introduction	1
2	**E-mail**	**6**
	What do the pupils get out of it?	6
	E-mail exchange models	7
	Choosing a language for communication	9
	Setting up an e-mail project	10
	Making the exchange work	11
	Creating a language portfolio	14
	Use of highlighting as a form of correction	15
	Coping with problems	18
	Other approaches to an e-mail exchange	21
3	**Notice boards**	**27**
	Features of notice boards	27
	Choosing a notice board provider	29
	Using a notice board for language learning	31
4	**Using messaging and chat rooms**	**40**
	Messaging	41
	Chat rooms	44
	Approaches to language learning using a chat room	47
	Mediating a chat room	52
5	**Integrating the four skills**	**53**
	Making audio links work	54
	Approaches to language learning through audio communication	58
	Supporting an audio exchange – how to talk	59
	Anticipating problems with spoken on-line communication in schools	59
	Making video links work	62
	Working in an on-line learning environment: a case study	66
6	Conclusion	68
	List of websites	**71**

1 Introduction

Ever since computers became small enough to be purchased by schools, the drive to include information technology in teaching and learning has increased steadily, leading first to the establishment of the National Grid for Learning (NGfL) and then to the current ICT in schools initiative (February 2004). Since the conception of the Internet, the opportunities over the last decade for communicating on-line have developed constantly, beginning with the very first e-mails and reaching the current standard of high-quality video conferencing. Since the first tentative e-mail exchanges in the early 1990s, a lot has happened. Now, pupils and teachers alike are theoretically able to communicate instantly both in written and in oral form with anybody around the world, provided they have access to the Internet and the same computer programs. The importance of communication with target language speaking communities is highlighted in the National Curriculum Programme of Study under the heading 'Developing cultural awareness':

4 Pupils should be taught about different countries and cultures by:
- *a working with authentic materials in the target language, including some from ICT-based sources;*
- *b communicating with native speakers;*
- *c considering their own culture and comparing it with the cultures of the countries and communities where the target language is spoken;*
- *d considering the experiences and perspectives of people in these countries and communities.*

Introduction

In addition to these intercultural elements, the possibilities this form of on-line communication holds for foreign language learning are immense, offering native speaker contact, authentic and age-relevant texts and information, opportunities for adapting language to different audiences, motivation resulting from 'real' communication, opportunities for independent and peer learning and the possibility to store, print and refer back to what has been learnt on-line. This message is clearly picked up in the National Strategy for Languages:

- *Teachers must harness the power of ICT to [...] provide access to a wider range of language experiences (p12).*
- *ICT can provide exposure to native speakers, it provides teaching opportunities that will engage many learners, in particular boys (p24).*
- *The social aspect of language communication can also be served through on-line discussion environments, text or audio, with learners or experts (p25).*

This book aims to explain the different technologies available and demonstrate how each can be exploited most effectively for language learning.

AN INTRODUCTION TO THE TERMINOLOGY

On-line communication began with e-mail, but it did not stop there. Throughout the book, the following forms of communication are examined:

- **E-mail:** the sending of messages electronically. Out of all the different types of communication this is the one closest to a letter format. It is possible to attach files to an e-mail, such as pictures, documents and sounds.
- **Notice boards:** posting a message to a website, where it will be displayed to allow other users to access and reply to it. Corresponding messages are displayed together in strands to ease reference.
- **Messaging:** similar to mobile phone texting, messaging programs allow users to send each other short messages which can be accessed either immediately or at a later date. Usually a messaging program appears in a small window on-screen and frequently a visual reminder (such as a flashing button) alerts the user that a new message has arrived.
- **Chat rooms:** either oral or written in style, a chat room is a program embedded in a website that allows a number of people to meet in real time

Communicating on-line

Introduction

on-line to 'chat'. Once users are logged in, they can see everything that other users type and/or hear everything other users say, allowing for communication between several people.
- **Video links:** the possibility to connect two or more users in such a way that they can not only talk to one another, but also see each other.

In principle, communication on-line falls into two categories, namely **asynchronous** and **synchronous**. Asynchronous exchanges are those that allow participants to prepare a message for the partner and post it, either via e-mail or on a notice board. This message can be retrieved at any time, making it unnecessary for both participants to be on-line at the same time. This provides a number of advantages for language learners:

- pupils can develop their skills of redrafting and focus on accuracy;
- dictionaries and other reference materials can be used to improve communication;
- pupils can develop their independence in using the target language at their own pace.

Asynchronous communication remains the most common, for a number of reasons:

- because of the time allowed for preparation, even beginning language learners can participate successfully in this form of exchange;
- the preparation time allows pupils to send messages that reflect their best possible linguistic ability, as they can check vocabulary, spellings and phrase structures;
- the preparation time also allows pupils to work more creatively and imaginatively;
- managing the challenge of getting two groups of exchange pupils on-line at the same time for synchronous communication proves to be difficult for many schools;
- asynchronous communication frequently takes place via e-mail, still the most familiar form of exchange and tends therefore to be favoured most by schools, teachers and learners alike.

Asynchronous communication is usually in the written format, whereas synchronous communication can be either written or oral. When participating in synchronous communication, all pupils involved will need to be on-line

Introduction

simultaneously, a challenge even within Europe, but nearly impossible to manage when the French-speaking exchange pupils live in Canada, for example. However, synchronous communication should not be dismissed easily, as it opens up completely new avenues for a language exchange:

- pupils will learn to think more quickly: they have to interpret what they see and hear on the spot, and use language in a creative and spontaneous way;
- the immediacy of communication requires pupils to take more risks with the language they know, accelerating the learning process;
- pupils may internalise vocabulary more effectively, enabling them to discuss issues and become used to thinking on their feet and defending their opinion;
- in oral communication with the aid of an audio link, pupils can practise their pronunciation with a native speaker and develop both their oral discussion skills and a more natural intonation;
- as it is easy to combine oral and written synchronous communication, pupils have the opportunity to practise all four skills together, supplementing oral discussions with written questions, explanations and peer correction where necessary or appropriate.

THE STRUCTURE OF THIS BOOK

This book takes a closer look at the opportunities for communication the Internet has to offer, giving advice on where to find suitable programs and how to use them in a foreign language teaching context. Each chapter covers a specific form of on-line communication, beginning with e-mail, then moving on to notice boards, messaging, text-based chat rooms and finally moving on to opportunities for integrating oral communication using oral chat rooms and video links. Throughout the book the advantages and disadvantages of each communication method are highlighted, giving teachers the chance to evaluate which method will be most suitable for their individual learning and teaching environment. Where appropriate there are 'How to ...' boxes, giving practical advice on generic technical and logistical issues, such as how to set up a notice board, using a messaging facility, creating an on-line learning environment, etc.

SECURITY AND SAFETY MATTERS

Introduction

It is difficult to be certain that the on-line communication pupils are engaging in is safe, especially if they are participating in on-line discussions in open chat rooms or sign up for e-mail friends from an unverified source. Because of the issues surrounding this, many schools routinely bar pupils from accessing communication facilities on-line by inserting a firewall into the school's Internet access which will stop any attempts by pupils to reach websites and programs that would allow them to contact other people on-line. This firewall, however, is flexible, allowing technicians to release access to sites specified by staff if they are needed for the pupils' learning process. Specific safety issues related to each form of communication are discussed throughout the book and suggestions made to minimise risk. Several sites on the Internet deal exclusively with safety on-line, giving general information which goes beyond the capacity of this book. Two of these sites are the Department for Education and Skills' 'Superhighway safety' website (**http://safety.ngfl.gov.uk**), which offers advice to schools, parents and on-line managers, and a website created as part of the Safer Use of Services on the Internet (SUSI) project involving several European countries and supported by the European Union Safer Internet Action Plan (**www.besafeonline.org**).

SUPPORTING WEBSITE

A Web page has been created on the CILT website, listing addresses for all the websites mentioned in the book at **www.cilt.org.uk/publications/communicatingonline.** From there you can follow live links through to the relevant Web pages mentioned in the book. This information will be updated from time to time as resources change location. A full listing of the websites mentioned in the book is also provided in the Website addresses (pp71–72).

Readers might also be interested in two further CILT publications: *InfoTech 3: WWW – The Internet* (Atkinson, T. 2002) and *New Pathfinder 3: Impact on learning – What ICT can bring to MFL in KS3* (Dugard, C. and Hewer, S. 2003). Both books contain further advice on how to successfully implement on-line learning in the MFL classroom.

2 E-mail

Despite the advent of more sophisticated possibilities, e-mailing remains the most frequent form of communication via the Internet, and rightly so. Using e-mails to maintain contact with and learn from a native speaker of another language is arguably closest to the already established penfriend schemes many schools participate in, yet it offers many additional opportunities for the language teacher and learner. This chapter gives an outline of what an e-mail exchange might consist of, plus hints and tips for teachers planning to set up an exchange.

WHAT DO THE PUPILS GET OUT OF IT?

In general, most pupils today will have had access to e-mail at some time or another and you may find that they will be fairly sophisticated in their use of e-mail. However, few will have used e-mail specifically to communicate in a foreign language. The skills related to this form of exchange, ranging from using accents, highlighting text and attaching further data, for example, provide useful development of the general ICT training pupils receive related to the use of e-mail. Occasionally pupils may wish to expand on their use of features and it could give these pupils a great confidence boost to introduce their ideas to the entire class. As far as whole-school benefits are concerned, e-mail poses no further cost to a school that is already connected to the Internet, making it possible to enable large numbers of pupils to get in contact with a native speaker.

When it comes to the linguistic benefits, the flexibility of e-mail has a lot to offer:

- Speedier than an exchange by letter, e-mail still demands use of stylistic nuances as in any other written medium, providing opportunities for pupils to exchange both short messages and carefully planned 'letters'.

E-mail

- The same advantage of speed also allows for quick replies to follow-up questions, allowing an exchange to gather momentum and gain in relevance – because of this, pupils can be more easily encouraged to direct questions to the exchange partner rather than the teacher, thus encouraging independent and peer learning.
- As it is likely that the e-mail exchange partner will be of a similar age, pupils are exposed to authentic language input, which also encourages them to closely examine their own language use, raising language awareness both in their mother tongue and the target language.
- Pupils can exploit e-mail features to facilitate communication, e.g. by highlighting or changing the layout of a text to emphasise opinions or mistakes.
- Teachers can choose to facilitate the pupils' exchanges by providing differentiated electronic writing frames in Word, with phrases and structures which the pupils may adapt to create their own exchange – this makes e-mail a suitable form of writing for any level of ability – alternatively, and similar to more conventional writing tasks, an e-mail may be prepared by the teacher, leaving only a few gaps for pupils to fill in. Such use of a writing frame allows for differentiation and makes it possible to use e-mail communication early on in the language-learning process.
- Where necessary, pupils can send multiple copies of their e-mails without any additional effort – this feature allows for the teacher to be copied in to an exchange, making it easier to keep track of the pupils' work. Alternatively, it allows for an e-mail exchange between more than two pupils who can keep track of the communication by sending messages to all participants.
- A record of the exchange can be kept, either by printing out messages or by saving them electronically. E-mail messages are automatically given a time and date stamp, allowing pupils or teachers to refer back to and assess the learning process that took place as part of the exchange.
- The electronic nature of e-mail text means that it can be copied, pasted and edited, making it possible for pupils to create a final document based on numerous exchanges (such as a project), which could then be printed and filed, submitted or displayed.

E-MAIL EXCHANGE MODELS

When planning an e-mail exchange, teachers have the opportunity to choose from a number of models, such as:

E-mail

- a whole-class exchange with an existing partner class abroad – schools that already have a partner school may find it useful to give each class one particular partner class abroad. Within the two paired classes, pupils work either individually or in small groups, depending on pupils' ability and intended outcomes;
- one-to-one exchange with a partner school abroad – once more, there is an existing partner school which can be taken advantage of for the exchange, but pupils are communicating voluntarily and largely in their own time;
- one-to-one exchanges with partners found via an agency (both within lesson time and as an additional spare-time activity) – there are several e-mail partnership agencies (discussed below), which will organise partner addresses for pupils;
- several classes from different countries using e-mail to collaborate on a project – this type of project, due to its size, requires a substantial amount of planning, but agencies such as the European School Network (www.eun.org) and the British Council's Windows on the World website (www.wotw.org.uk) often help with finding partner classes;
- group-to-group exchanges within two partner classes – within this type of exchange, pupils may work in individual pairings, but have a 'buddy pair' to call on for mutual support. This encourages peer work as well as independent learning. Alternatively, small groups may be paired with a similar-sized group in the partner class, each subgroup working on one aspect of a larger topic. At the end of a specified period, the work from each subgroup is combined into a larger project – a display, book of stories, etc.

It is possible to adopt one of these models or combine one with another, depending on class size and ability. Within the chosen model there are a range of approaches you can take, ranging from penfriendships to structured project-focused exchanges. The exchange models can be applied to projects of any length. For example, a long-term exchange might be based on an e-mail penfriend scheme supported with tasks and projects. On the other hand, a research project requiring native-speaker input on a certain topic would limit the exchange to an agreed period of time. Again, the flexibility of exchange model, approach and timespan make an e-mail exchange a viable option for most schools.

In addition to actual exchanges, e-mail can also be used to do research by writing to theatres, museums, clubs, etc, requesting information. Again, pupils can either

E-mail

do so individually or in groups, preparing for GCSE oral topics, an exchange, or gathering information for a whole-class project that will be collated and presented at the end of the project period (see 'Using e-mail for researching information, p21).

As mentioned above, there are agencies which are able to find partners for pupils, such as the tandem agency (**tandem@slf3.slf.ruhr-uni-bochum.de**). Most of these agencies are not necessarily equipped to research addresses to guarantee their authenticity. Schools advertising on the European School Network (**www.eun.org**) also do not always display a readily recognisable school e-mail address – doing a search for the school on the Internet and giving them a quick phone call to verify names of staff members may therefore be the safest way to ensure the authenticity of e-mail addresses.

CHOOSING A LANGUAGE FOR COMMUNICATION

There are a number of possible combinations when it comes to choosing which language to use for communication, namely:

- giving information in the foreign language and asking questions in the mother tongue – most pupils begin to learn a foreign language by giving information and neglecting the art of questioning – using this approach, pupils are exposed to good examples of question formats from their native speaker partner, allowing their lesser developed skills to catch up;
- starting off by writing everything that can be said in the foreign language, then giving additional information in the mother tongue (this can be motivating for very communicative pupils who get annoyed by their own lack of communicative competence, but can also result in frustration at the returned e-mail which may well contain long stretches of writing at a high level in the foreign language);
- keeping to one language per e-mail and switching for the next (all English the first, French the second, English the third, etc) – pupils take it in turns to be the 'expert', rather than having to switch their attention between the two languages, which some pupils may find very challenging;
- writing in the mother tongue initially, and gradually introducing the foreign language over time;
- both partners asking questions and receiving answers in the target language so that answers are always given in the language of the question, e.g. the

E-mail

UK-based pupils ask questions in Spanish and receive a reply to that question in Spanish, and the Spanish pupils write a question in English requiring a response from the UK-based pupils in English. To ensure that the exchange gives ample practice in writing in the target language as well as reading authentic material, it is important that pupils work towards a written outcome such as a report or PowerPoint presentation which can be sent to their partner for peer correction;
- using one of these combinations, with the exchange culminating in a written outcome in the target language, as described in the previous point.

Each of these approaches has its advantages and disadvantages and it is therefore down to individual teachers to find the one which they think will be best for their class. The one approach deliberately not mentioned above is that of both pupils writing exclusively in their foreign language (the English pupil writing only Spanish, the Spanish pupil writing only English). Although this approach remains very common, it does mean that pupils lose out on the opportunity of reading the foreign language as it is written by a native speaker – missing out on increasing their passive knowledge of the language, which would, over time, filter into their own target language use. Furthermore, having to labour over each and every sentence can make the idea of having a partner seem a chore, and communication can stagnate at a rather low level (i.e. that of the foreign language for both partners) and most exchanges will prove not to be very exciting.

SETTING UP AN E-MAIL PROJECT

Before embarking on an e-mail project, the teachers involved will need to agree on the following points:

- Length and purpose of project
- Form of exchange
- Language
- Working with material.

Length and purpose of project

Will the exchange last a month, term, year or Key Stage? Are the pupils going to be exchanging e-mails as a communicative exercise or will there be a more

specific, measurable outcome such as a presentation, a questionnaire, a display? How will the success of the project be determined?

Form of exchange

What access do the pupils have? How many e-mails a week/month will they be able to send? Will there be a specified length to e-mails? Which e-mail addresses will be used? (See 'Solving security issues' on p19.) Will teachers need to monitor outgoing messages and – if so – how? Will the pupils be able to send attachments, such as picture files and documents?

Language

Which language will the pupils be working in? (See 'Choosing a language for communication' on p9.) Will teachers intervene to ensure high levels of accuracy?

Working with material

How will pupils assemble what they have found? Are they asked to keep a language portfolio (see below), save e-mails, reply within a specified time span, make notes of their findings, keep a learner's diary, etc? Will they need additional access to computers outside lesson time and, if so, how can they get it?

MAKING THE EXCHANGE WORK

Quality of language used

Just as with classroom learning, an e-mail exchange will benefit from a set of regulations and structured ideas. The actual exchange may take place without the teacher being physically present. Rules, therefore, can serve to remind the learner of what it is they wish to achieve. One area in which an understanding needs to be reached between teachers is in the quality of language used. The language engaged in during on-line communication frequently resembles that of text messaging and this can be detrimental to accurate language learning (unless a study of text messaging in different countries is the topic of conversation). More often than not the partner at the other end will wish to improve their English, just as the UK-based learner will want to improve their

E-mail

knowledge of the foreign language. Both learners will therefore need to use accurate language (to the best of their ability) to enable the partner to model their foreign language use against that of the native speaker.

A common approach towards an e-mail exchange is that the partner will serve as an interim 'tutor', flagging up mistakes made by the language learner. If this is the case, the learners will need to specify what mistakes they wish to have pointed out to them – a general approach here will result in far too much work for both partners (especially at the early stages of language learning) and a rather depressing number of mistakes being returned to the learner. Initially – and depending on the individual foreign language – capital letters, accents, verb position and verb conjugation make a good focus that can then develop into specific ideas tailor-made for each individual learner. A list of mistakes to concentrate on should be part of the language portfolio. Teachers of younger pupils may wish to ask pupils to keep a reminder of the rules in their folder, similar to the example shown here.

This approach is developed further in the context of the e-Tandem project (see p25).

My e-mail exchange

I will:
- keep a record of all e-mails I'm sending and receiving;
- make notes when I come across a word I don't know and look it up or ask my partner;
- always write good English, so my partner can depend on what I'm writing because it is correct;
- do my best to write well in the foreign language and ask my partner if I have any problems;
- go to my teacher if I have a problem my partner can't help me with.

These are the problems I would like my partner to help me with:
_____
_____

These are the problems my partner would like help with:
_____
_____

INFOT_eCH
Communicating on-line

E-mail

Guiding the content

It is important for language beginners that any exchange includes a structured task, as pupils often do not see the opportunities for communication, resulting in a 'Hi, I'm fine, how are you? Bye' form of exchange. By giving detailed instructions at the beginning, pupils can have the motivating experience of composing e-mails of considerable length. These instructions can be given in the mother tongue or the foreign language, or even a combination of the two. As support materials can be supplied electronically, pupils can copy and paste phrases to help them construct their messages. Below are several examples for instructions for e-mails in varying stages of an exchange.

Here are some ideas for your first e-mail. The questions you could ask your partner are already written in German:

Say what you are called.	*Wie heißt du?*
Say how old you are.	*Wie alt bist du?*
Say where you live.	*Wo wohnst du?*
Say what you look like.	*Wie siehst du aus?*
Say whether you've got any brothers or sisters.	*Hast du Geschwister?*
Say whether you've got any pets.	*Hast du ein Haustier?*

In English, describe some of your family members. Make sure you check your spellings in both languages, otherwise your partner may find it difficult to understand you.

In French, tell your partner about how you spent last weekend. Say where you went, what you did, who came with you and what you liked and disliked about the weekend. Give as much information as possible. If there is something you can't say in French, add it in English at the end of the e-mail – you can ask your partner to help you write it in French. You could also tell your partner what your perfect weekend would be like and ask what he or she was doing last weekend.

INFOTECH
Communicating on-line

E-mail

> Start a discussion about a healthy lifestyle – think about the Spanish vocabulary you already know, to do with food and exercise. Here are a few phrases to help you:
>
> | | |
> |---|---|
> | I find ... unnecessary. | *Encuentro ... poco necesario.* |
> | I find ... unhealthy. | *Encuentro ... poco sano.* |
> | We should all do/eat more ... | *Todos deberíamos hacer/comer más ...* |
> | Too many people don't ... | *Demasiada gente no ...* |
> | People today eat more ... and less ... than 50 years ago. | *La gente de hoy come más ... y menos ... que hace 50 anos.* |
>
> What does your partner think? Make sure you ask questions, either in English or Spanish, that will bring out their opinion.

These sample tasks invite the learner to use a combination of both languages. While the first one only encourages pupils to be careful about their work, it does establish good working habits, which is particularly useful as e-mails are so frequently used in everyday life. The third task openly invites collaboration between the partners, while keeping the topic more general. At this point, it could be presumed that pupils have already participated in the exchange over a period of several weeks or months, therefore necessitating only a quick reminder to ask for help and to engage the partner in the communication by asking questions.

CREATING A LANGUAGE PORTFOLIO

E-mails can be stored, edited and printed, making it possible for pupils to gradually assemble a language portfolio which enables both them and the teacher to retrace their path of language learning throughout the exchange. For example, a language portfolio can not only be used by the teacher to assess the frequency of contact, but it also shows how the language-learning partners make use of their time together. In this way, a language portfolio offers a way of evaluating the success of the e-mail exchange, but also allows pupils to go back over their learning at a much later date. Depending on the type of exchange, a language portfolio should show that the pupil critically engages with the

language. While a lot of this critical engagement can be shown as part of the e-mail itself (see 'Use of highlighting' below), the language portfolio could also be used to store draft e-mails which have been reworked before they have been sent, notes by the pupil relating to vocabulary, personal learning goals, etc. See the eTandem example (see p25), for a project which makes extensive use of the portfolio.

USE OF HIGHLIGHTING AS A FORM OF CORRECTION

E-mails today are very much the equivalent of Word documents in that they allow the writer to use many of the features initially reserved for word processing. This, in turn, makes opportunities for correction much easier to handle. Not only is it possible to colour code mistakes (e.g. green for capital letters, pink for verb position), it also makes it easier in general for language learners to see where they are going wrong. If printing in black and white, using different fonts for different mistakes would be a useful alternative. The example on p16 illustrates such practice, concentrating on capital letters, umlauts and one specific spelling mistake, leaving other mistakes 'unnoticed' in order to minimise frustration. As long as pupils are clear that not all mistakes will be picked up by their partner, there should be no problems arising from this practice – after all, the pupils can ask each other about specific sentences if they wish to do so.

Usually, pupils enjoy correcting one another, but they will need to understand the importance of what they are doing, as the partner might not actually understand what it is they have done wrong. While pupils cannot be expected to be able to teach their own language, the responsibility for their partner enforces the need to try their best to use correct language themselves at all times. Another issue is positive criticism – more often than not, pupils are already very good at encouraging one another (mainly with more or less truthful statements such as 'your English is much better than my German/Spanish', etc). These general statements can be channelled into positive feedback regarding specific points and pupils should be encouraged to mention to their partners particularly good sentences or use of vocabulary.

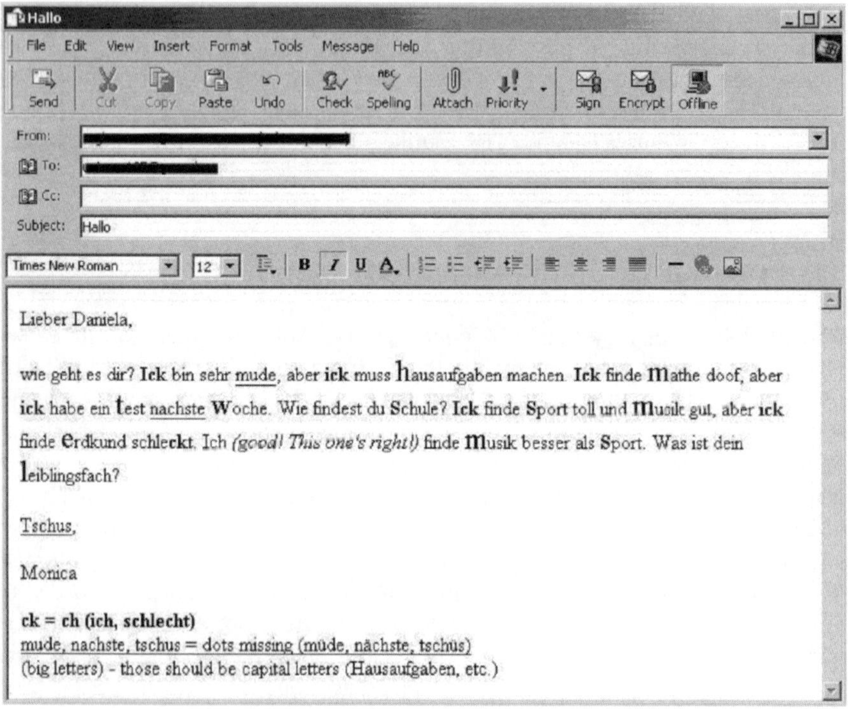

E-mail

![Outlook Express email window screenshot]

Subject: Hallo

Lieber Daniela,

wie geht es dir? Ick bin sehr mude, aber ick muss hausaufgaben machen. Ick finde mathe doof, aber ick habe ein test nachste Woche. Wie findest du Schule? Ick finde Sport toll und musik gut, aber ick finde erdkund schleckt. Ich *(good! This one's right!)* finde musik besser als Sport. Was ist dein leiblingsfach?

Tschus,

Monica

ck = ch (ich, schlecht)
mude, nachste, tschus = dots missing (müde, nächste, tschüs)
(big letters) - those should be capital letters (Hausaufgaben, etc.)

NB: *This example uses Outlook Express, and not all e-mail programs have the same features. In some cases, using a Word attachment may be necessary to convey all points clearly.*

Some school computers may automatically format e-mails in a way which loses fonts and accents. Technical support should be able to help here. If not, sending e-mails as .rtf file attachments may work better, or other systems (use of asterisks, brackets, etc) could be developed.

Communicating on-line

E-mail

Supplementing e-mail messages

Attaching additional files to e-mail messages gives pupils yet another opportunity to embellish on real, meaningful conversations they are having with their partners. Imagine the motivation and illumination of meaning when a short piece of writing about '*Ma maison*' is accompanied by a number of pictures of different rooms, or when '*Meine Familie*' includes a family photo and a personal introduction includes a short sound file with the pronunciation of the name. In most exchanges these attachments will be pictures or perhaps sounds, but there are further possibilities, such as PowerPoint presentations or Word files. While there is not enough space here to discuss fully all aspects of attachments, it should be mentioned that sounds and pictures in particular can greatly increase the size of an e-mail and most e-mail accounts have a file size limit on incoming messages. Also, many schools in Britain and abroad have introduced firewalls to their systems which will prevent any e-mails with attachments from getting through. This is due to a fear of viruses and it is important here to liaise with technical staff and teachers abroad at the receiving schools to find out what individual school regulations are and to make any possible adjustments.

One very useful application of this facility is the exchange of PowerPoint presentations. A possible project leading towards a PowerPoint presentation may look like this:

- Pupils prepare a presentation on their hometown (or indeed, the partner's hometown). They use e-mails to write fully formulated sentences relating to this presentation.
- Each partner creates PowerPoint slides, using bullet points and pictures to prompt the use of full sentences when speaking in front of the class.
- The presentation is mailed back and forth with comments until both partners agree that the information is accurate both in content and language.
- This presentation is then given in front of the class (where possible), or even to the partner class via videoconferencing.

This way of working develops useful language-learning skills, namely:

- allowing the pupils to get into the habit of returning to material and reworking it;
- listening to the advice of other people;
- developing awareness of the target language culture in the context of both the topic and peer communication;

INFOTECH
Communicating on-line

E-mail

- establishing contact with a native speaker;
- developing an understanding of PowerPoint and its technical facilities as a presentation tool;
- giving pupils the opportunity to develop speaking skills with the support of pictures and bullet points.

For a lot of students preparing for GCSE examinations, the oral presentation is one of the hardest aspects to master. With a project such as the one above, they are given the opportunity to develop and practise skills in a motivating and non-threatening, yet authentic environment.

Inserting foreign accents

Often, e-mail programmes themselves offer no way of inserting foreign accents. The solution here is to compose the e-mail in Word and then to copy and paste it into an e mail, where it will hopefully display correctly. You can also try using the character map for producing accents directly into an e-mail (go to Start>Programs>Accessories). Attachments are one way of ensuring that foreign accents actually arrive intact. Although e-mail programs today are set to display accents accurately, some individual computers may still turn a 'ñ' into 'RL//6%' – very annoying when pupils are trying to learn a foreign language. Technical support should be able to solve the problem but, in the meantime, one way to circumvent the problem is to type out the e-mails in Word, save them as an .rtf file and attach them to an e-mail.

COPING WITH PROBLEMS

As with any other teaching which involves technology or people from outside the school, things can and will go wrong. Partnerships will stall, the computer room will be unavailable at a crucial time, there will be an uneven number of pupils in a class-to-class exchange, the pupils will match each other in age, but not ability (or vice versa), a computer virus can cause the school to put a halt to all on-line communication, etc. The list of possible problems is endless and, unfortunately, a lot of them can have a detrimental effect on an exchange, particularly if this exchange stretches over a certain length of time. Below are detailed a number of problems with suggestions for possible solutions. As technical problems can be very specific to individual schools and cannot be

covered in full here, we suggest that you approach internal ICT staff with any problems unrelated to the actual language-learning process.

Solving security issues

The e-mail address pupils use can tell potential partners a lot about who they are talking to. While this is not a problem in official school-to-school exchanges, a school e-mail address means that the pupils are easily recognised as being of school age, which can be undesirable in open e-mail exchanges arranged by an agency. Unless all addresses are entered by school officials only, no agency will be able to guarantee absolute security and this should be kept in mind. As a general rule, it is recommended that e-mail addresses give no indication of age, gender or location – all this information forms part of the communication process at a later date.

While a school-based e-mail address has the advantage of enabling the teacher to keep track of the number of e-mails exchanged, it also requires pupils to engage in the exchange only during school hours and from the school premises. This requires a lot of organisation if there isn't enough lesson time to devote to the project and if pupils are relied on to bring in prepared e-mail replies for their partner. If you have pupils with access to the Internet from home and want them to continue their exchange over the weekends and holidays, you should ensure that they have a personal Web-based e-mail address from a provider such as Yahoo! or Hotmail. However, some schools have a network policy which bars access to these Web-based e-mail providers. In this case, enquiries need to be made as to whether it will be possible to allow the exchange participants access, or whether a school address must be used.

Uneven numbers in a class-to-class exchange

Uneven class numbers require uneven pairings, two-to-one or even three-to-one. When working in larger groups, pupils should ensure all pupils receive a copy of their communications by 'carbon copying' (cc) other recipients into the e-mail. Teachers will need to keep a close eye on these partnerships to ensure each pupil has an equal chance to participate. Pairing several UK-based pupils to communicate with one pupil abroad can give weaker pupils the chance to share the workload, whereas allocating one of your pupils to two pupils abroad can provide differentiation for able pupils.

E-mail

Stalling partnerships

Should communication stall in a class-to-class exchange, contact the member of staff abroad and work on the problem from both ends. Partners may be sick (in which case it may be possible to arrange for access to e-mail at their home or have a printout brought over by a friend), or simply have left the school. If all partnerships have been arranged individually, there are really only two options: either place the 'abandoned' pupils with an existing partnership, to form a three, or find a new partner for him or her. Neither option is ideal – the existing partnership may well feel annoyed by the 'intrusion' of another person and, in both cases, with a new partner entering the relationship communication must in part go back to the beginning. On the plus side, a weak pupil may benefit from being allowed to start over again with a new partner, revisiting useful vocabulary, structures and information, whereas they would possibly take a very passive role if placed within an existing partnership. One way around the general problem is to arrange all partnerships as part of a larger study group, which can 'catch' lost partners in case of absence and/or sickness. By creating these types of 'buddy groups' pupils benefit not only from having a 'substitute partner' in case of absence, but are also able to mutually support each other throughout their work.

Uneven age/linguistic/technical ability

Most pupils on the continent start language lessons much earlier than those in the UK, which can lead to some very uneven partnerships indeed. Similarly, variations in age and technical ability can lead to demotivation and frustration. Discussion of these issues by the two teachers involved at the planning stage is crucial, so that adjustments can be made and expectations properly managed. For example, it could be agreed that the length of message pupils should aim for be set differently for the two schools. Or pupils could be put into groups, with the teacher making sure that there is enough technical and linguistic expertise as well as maturity within each group. If the pupils are willing to help each other, these problems solve themselves – appealing to a pupil's sense of maturity may help. If, for some reason, the problem becomes insurmountable, swapping partners with another pupil (in a class-to-class situation) or finding a new partner (in an individual situation) may be the only way forward.

E-mail

School system crash

If the whole computer network is down, teachers should phone or e-mail each other from home to let one another know the problem and when the exchange may continue. In the meantime, pupils can prepare future communication by researching or making notes. If it is only the Internet connection that is down, the group's e-mails can be collated in a lesson and sent to the other school at a later time or from outside school.

Some pupils do not receive a reply

This is often a case of 'best-laid plans': the computer room is booked, the class is in, eager to work on the exchange, they log on, retrieve their e-mails ... only to find their partner hasn't replied. If the pupils are part of a larger 'buddy group', this isn't too much of a problem, as each pupil can easily be linked with somebody from the same study group to reply to another pupil, although the sense of disappointment will linger. If the pupils are paired individually, it will be worth the pupil composing a reminder for his or her partner (supported by an e-mail between the two teachers). Also, remind the pupils that their partner might be ill or otherwise absent, in which case an e-mail from their partner might be just the thing to cheer them up.

Pupils must know that they can turn to their 'on-line learning advisor' if they have a problem, whether this is their classroom teacher or another member of staff overseeing an exchange outside lesson time. Over time, problems will become routine and both pupils and staff will become adept in dealing with them, or even avoiding them in the first place.

OTHER APPROACHES TO AN E-MAIL EXCHANGE

In addition to the class-to-class exchange illustrated above, here are a few further examples which may work in different settings.

Using e-mail for researching information

Writing letters to obtain information remains an important skill in the curriculum, but practice can seem irrelevant as pupils may never need to book a train ticket in real life, for example. However, e-mail does give them the

E-mail

opportunity to research and communicate with 'the real world' in a time-efficient way. Opportunities include writing to tourist information centres requesting information about the local area, enquiring about concert programmes, requesting a local map or information on GCSE topics. This is also an excellent source of authentic material for either the pupils themselves or the department in general, to be used in future years. This type of research via e-mail differs from research on the Internet in that it is interactive and involves at least a basic level of communication – even if a request is not met with a written reply on top of any sent material, the pupils will have rehearsed the appropriate language in a real context.

Teachers of KS4 classes preparing for a trip abroad might decide to hand over the gathering of information and planning for the trip to the pupils themselves, who will thereby gain a greater sense of ownership regarding the trip. Working in groups on different elements of the trip, an initial Internet search could ascertain what there is to do in the area, followed by more detailed research on concert dates or exhibition prices via e-mail messages to sources of information in the target language country. After gathering the information, these groups can then report back to the class in the target language, introducing an oral element to the research process. While this can definitely be a very long-winded approach to planning a trip, the sense of ownership can more than make up for it. For less independent or younger classes, it is possible to introduce the pupils to the itinerary, then divide them into groups and ask them to contact the relevant amusement parks, art galleries, schools, etc for information. The trick to receiving a personal reply here is to ask direct questions which will entice somebody at the other end to hit the reply button, rather than simply to send a brochure – a request for 'information' will often result in your being directed to their website. If the pupils are aiming for more personal replies, it can often be beneficial to admit that they are pupils and researching for a class project. If the class will be visiting a certain museum while abroad, for example, it would be possible to ask for suggestions on how long a visit they should plan for and even to ask if it might be possible to meet with a museum employee during their visit, which in turn enables the class to prepare questions for the actual visit in advance. As museums are there for educational purposes, they are often particularly helpful.

Story writing via e-mail

Story writing often holds a fascination for pupils, mainly because it is a release from highly structured curricular content and lets the imagination run free. In MFL lessons, however, story-writing activities can be rare, for fear that pupils will abandon all grammatical care and simply translate word for word from English into the foreign language, resulting in paragraphs of gibberish. Where an e-mail exchange focuses on writing a story, pupils can work more independently from the teacher in the knowledge that the partner abroad will highlight problems as they arise, simply because he or she cannot understand what the partner produces. By 'bouncing' a story back and forth, the pupils are therefore able to correct each other as they are meant to do in a usual exchange, while continuing the thread of the story. Secondly, a text needs to be of signficant length to incorporate a beginning, middle or end, so writing a complete story on one's own can be a daunting task. Sharing the work with a partner or groups of pupils can relieve the pressure and heighten interest.

Story writing via e-mail can function in a number of ways, based on the number of people involved and the languages used. In a long-term exchange, it may be possible to write several stories, changing the language for each one, to ensure that both sides benefit linguistically from the exchange. On a smaller scale, for one story, it should be possible to swap paragraph by paragraph. Pupils will enjoy this linguistic 'mess', although the younger ones particularly will need guidance with their writing. Depending on how much text is expected from the pupils each time, sections of the story can be prepared in advance and checked by the teacher if desired, before being copied into an e-mail and sent. Older pupils should be able to correct each other as described above.

A whole group story can be desirable when teachers wish to avoid having to spend a substantial amount of time on the story, or wish to make use of the motivational aspect of story writing to keep the overall exchange going. The story begins with a group of three or so pupils, who begin the story in their mother tongue (mainly because story beginnings can be notoriously difficult). The group then aims to include detail in the foreign language – a physical description, siblings, etc. This story beginning then gets sent (either via the teacher or directly) to the class abroad, who will read it to their class, correct any mistakes and work in the same manner – developing the actual thread of the story in the respective mother tongue, but adding details in the target language. A big issue when writing stories is that of tense; teachers may wish to insist that younger pupils

E-mail

write in the present tense – this will feel unusual to the pupils, so any beginnings such as 'once upon a time, there was ...' will need to be firmly redirected to the present. Stories can be a good way to introduce the past tense, however. As a general rule, pupils could be allowed to use past and future references in their mother tongue, sticking to the present tense in the target language, until they are comfortable enough to switch. If pupils are unsure how to start, giving them a choice of beginnings can be helpful – either in English or in the target language – see the box below for ideas.

> Tina is getting up – late, yet again. She can hear her mother shout from downstairs, telling her to hurry. She drags herself out of bed and into the bathroom. A quick examination in the mirror: *Tina hat lange rote Haare und braune Augen. Sie ist ziemlich klein und schlank, und sie findet ihre Nase zu groß. Ihre Schwester Natalie hat eine kleine Nase, aber keine roten Haare. Tina hat lieber rote Haare als eine kleine Nase.* She sighs. 'I'm coming, Mum', she yells, struggling into her clothes. She rushes downstairs.

> David opens the door to his new house for the first time – he didn't want to move house, lose his friends, start a new school. *'Maman, où est ma chambre?' dit-il. 'Au premier étage', dit sa mère. David monte l'escalier, et il trouve sa chambre. Elle est grande, mais il n'y a pas de meubles ... 'Maman, où sont les meubles?'* David's Mum comes up after him. 'I don't know', she says. 'They should be here ... oh dear!'

> Elena wanders down the street thinking of nothing in particular, when suddenly she sees a dog tied to a lamp post. *Elena ve el perro. El perro es pequeño y tímido. Parece triste. ¿Qué pasa?* Elena goes up to the dog and strokes it. 'I'm going to take care of you', she says, when ...

All these beginnings make an attempt to introduce more complicated language in the mother tongue, drawing their attention to verbs and narrative vocabulary such as 'suddenly' and 'yet again', while keeping the target language very simple. Initially, pupils may find this manner of writing difficult, but they will learn quickly, especially if they are given the chance to feed back to the class and discuss any developments.

Through the practice of reporting back to the class, the pupils can keep track of the story and discuss any language that comes up, to ensure that when it is their turn, they will be able to continue the plot. Furthermore, the reporting gives the teacher a chance to see how the class is doing without having to make 'official' enquiries which might distract from the 'fun' of the activity, turning it into work.

Once the story is finished, the communication need not stop – the story can be put on the school website (or the pupils may wish to create a website of their own to document their exchange), it can be read out to other classes or at assembly, or illustrated with pictures and stored in the school library – once more, pupils can gain a sense of 'owning' their lessons and having real input into their learning.

The 'eTandem' project

eTandem language learning involves two partners from different countries collaborating via an e-mail exchange specifically to further their own and each other's linguistic and cultural knowledge. The pupils are encouraged to engage in the e-mail exchange outside lessons, although the project may just as easily be incorporated into lesson time. Partnerships are arranged by the eTandem agency, which tries to keep in mind requests regarding age and gender. Their e-mail address is **tandem@slf3.slf.ruhr-uni-bochum.de**.

eTandem operates mainly on two principles, that of autonomy and that of reciprocity. Pupils are responsible for their own learning and that of their partner, and are encouraged to correct each other and take the time to answer questions carefully, even discussing the process of language learning itself with their partners. At the same time, pupils are asked to spend 50% of their time available in each language – if they have half an hour at their disposal, they are likely to begin by writing for fifteen minutes in the foreign language, then spend fifteen minutes in their mother tongue. In this way, beginning language learners will receive only a short excerpt in their mother tongue (which they are encouraged to correct and discuss with their partner), while being introduced to a long excerpt in the foreign language which exposes them to vocabulary and sentence structures. Over time, as the pupils gain confidence in the target language, this difference in length will begin to even out.

Although pupils are free to discuss anything they want, the originators of eTandem are aware that sometimes communication may stall, which is why there are a number of suggested tandem tasks pupils can follow available on the Internet

E-mail

at **www.slf.ruhr-uni-bochum.de/etandem/kultur/english/index.html**. Pupils also keep a language portfolio of their e-mails, vocabulary, learning goals and a learner's diary, which they use to discuss possible ways forward with the 'counsellor', a member of staff pupils can turn to with problems relating to their eTandem exchange.

Further information on eTandem can be found on the Internet, under **www.slf.ruhr-uni-bochum.de/etandem/etindex-en.html**.

Group-to-group exchange for research purposes (GCSE)

Instead of linking pupils individually within a class-to-class exchange, pupils can be split into groups to work on a project in collaboration with a group from the partner school. The teachers of both classes need to agree on a topic or project, such as a joint newspaper in English and French, a project studying environmental issues in both countries, posters around school displaying life in France for the European Day of Languages, etc, and what form the exchange should take (see 'Setting up an e-mail project' p10). Each group deals with a certain aspect of the overall project. Over a period agreed in advance, the pupils exchange e-mails regarding the topic of their research, as well as the structures and phrases they will need to write up their research. Pupils have a certain amount of time allocated each lesson to share their findings with their study group, discuss what the group will need next in the way of information and who will try to access which information. Once a fortnight, there is a whole class discussion to deal with problems and allow all participants to keep an overview of what is happening. This form of exchange allows the pupils to gain access to a wider range of linguistic input (due to the number of partners abroad and the scope of the topic covered within the class), and helps them to gain skills in planning, researching, sharing information and team work. After the specified period of time, groups write up their findings and share them with their own class and the class abroad, which makes final suggestions on changes in the language before the results of the project are published for others to see.

3 Notice boards

Having taken a look at e-mailing, the second possibility for asynchronous on-line communication outlined in this book is notice boards. A notice board does 'exactly what it says on the tin'. Notice boards offer a way to post messages onto a Web page, where they are accessible to other users who can read and reply to them. Messages are usually displayed chronologically, clearly outlining which message forms a reply to another one, making it easy to keep track of different strands in a conversation. Just as with an actual notice board, messages do not disappear after they have been read, so it is possible to refer back to older messages, following a thread from beginning to end. Due to their many advantages, notice boards now form an integral part of many distance-learning courses, and they also offer great potential for language learning. On the Web, notice boards can also be known as discussion forums, message boards, clubs or groups.

FEATURES OF NOTICE BOARDS

- One of the main advantages of notice boards is the idea of 'stranding' the messages. This makes it possible to see exactly which message attracted which replies, and in what order, enabling pupils as well as staff to follow a thread of communication without everybody being present simultaneously.
- On-screen, each message usually has a title, a time or date stamp and the name of the author. If another pupil chooses to reply to that message, they have the choice of keeping the same title, or changing it to something which serves their purpose better (e.g. the expression of an opinion, etc).

Notice boards

- Depending on the program, replies to a message may be indented, listed underneath the original message, or a number next to the message may indicate how many replies you find when you click on it (see below).

[screenshot of Yahoo group "vive_harry_potter - Vive Harry Potter" message list showing messages 893-902 dated Samedi 23/8/2003 and Dimanche 24/8/2003, with subjects including "Re: Traduction non officiel d'Harry Potter et l'Ordre du Phénix e", "Re: [vive_harry_potter] Traduction non officiel d'Harry Potter et l'", "Re: mon site sur harrypotter", and "[vive_harry_potter] Traduction non officiel d'Harry Potter et l'Ord"]

- Any pupil or teacher can read opinions and information and relate them to each individual participating.
- Some programs will allow attachments to be posted with messages, making it possible to display text files, pictures, photos, etc.
- As message board strands are usually retained on the Web for some time, learners have the chance to refer back to what has been said again and again, picking up points of discussion and accessing phrases and vocabulary long after they have been originally posted. At the same time, teachers get to see to what extent the pupils are engaging in the project, unlike when they are communicating by e-mail or in unmonitored chat rooms. In addition, teachers have the opportunity to guide a discussion subtly by posting messages themselves or drawing out comments from less able pupils.
- Not all schools allow access to notice boards, but this can be cleared with ICT staff, allowing pupils to view new messages from school and home.

Communicating on-line

Notice boards

- If the teacher has created the notice board (see the 'How to ...' box below for details on this), it is possible for him or her to remove inappropriate messages, as well as regulate access. From a security point of view, and because it is comparatively easy to do, it is therefore recommended that teachers **create** a notice board, rather than use an existing one where it is impossible to avoid potential risks to pupils. For further discussion of related issues, please see 'Using pre-exising noticeboards' on p32.

For a language-learning situation, these features combine into one of the best methods for on-line communication available. Any learning group can be started by the teacher, opening a strand such as 'introduce yourself', inviting members of the group to start telling the other participants about themselves. By replying to some of the messages with quick contributions ('I like going to the cinema, too! What's your favourite film?'), the teacher can introduce a more communicative element through leading by example, and encourage the learners to do the same. This is a good way to get any learning group started and further ideas on how to use notice boards for projects are discussed below in 'Using a notice board for language learning'.

CHOOSING A NOTICE BOARD PROVIDER

There are a multitude of notice boards already available, used by a varying number of clientele. Notice boards are set up and used by support groups, discussion forums, groups of friends and, indeed, language learners worldwide. One of the most prolific suppliers of free notice board services is Yahoo!, although the number of groups for any specific topic fluctuates enormously, making it nearly impossible to predict which will still be active after a few weeks or months.

The guidelines below refer to notice boards set up specifically by teachers for an exchange within a certain group. Yahoo! and other notice board providers list a number of open notice boards which are accessible to anyone. Please remember that security is not guaranteed on these notice boards.

Notice boards

How to ... start a notice board

It helps if you have a list of e-mail addresses for the pupils you would like to access the group – you will need it to invite them to join once you have set up the group (step 7 below).

① Go to **http://groups.yahoo.com**.

② If you are new to Yahoo! Messenger and notice boards, click on 'sign up as a new user' and follow the instructions on-screen (picking a user name that has no gender or age-related connotations. You may also wish to unclick all of Yahoo!'s friendly hints that mean they will bombard you with advertisement e-mails). At this point, you will also have to create the password that you need to verify under point 3.

③ Yahoo! will send a confirmation e-mail to the address you specified within seconds. You will need to click on the link they are sending you and verify your password. You are now registered.

④ Going back to the 'groups' main page, click on 'Start a new group' and select a category for your group. For languages, there are listings under 'Schools and Education > bilingual' and 'Schools and Education > By Subject > Languages'. Once you have found an appropriate category, click on 'Place my group in this category'.

⑤ Choose a name for your group and describe it. You could begin here by keeping the introduction bilingual to set a framework for future use of the notice board. Here, you are also given the chance to create and edit your 'profile', i.e. the information other people can find out about you if they search for your user name. Have a look at what they ask of you and decide for yourself if you want to provide that information, but remember that anything you enter will be accessible to everybody on the Internet. This also goes for profiles your pupils enter, so be sure to tell them this.

⑥ Once you click 'Continue', your group's Web address is displayed. This page also gives you the chance to 'Customize' your group. Click on this button, and you will find you can keep your group unlisted and grant access to invited participants only, allowing for security and privacy. Take a look at the other settings and choose those which best suit your purpose for the group.

⑦ You are now asked to invite group members by listing their e-mail addresses and to post a welcome message. Your pupils will receive this welcome e-mail with a link to click on to join the group.

Communicating on-line

Notice boards

⑧ Once your pupils click on the link, they will be given a choice about how they would like to receive the messages – some people have messages sent by e-mail, rather than accessing them on the Internet. Because you wish to exploit the stranding feature of the notice boards format, ignore the e-mail option.

⑨ A link will now take your pupils directly to the home page of your group. If they click on 'Messages' to the left of the screen, they will be able to see any messages posted, and will be able to add their own. It may be helpful for your pupils to save the address of the group as a 'favourite', so they can access it quickly every time they return.

⑩ Because you set up the notice board, you are known as the 'moderator', which will allow you to change any settings at a later date via the group's website.

As with all ideas mentioned in this book, using a notice board may be a problem if schools are automatically blocking access to all discussion forums. Again, it may be possible to allow access to individual sites only, which will enable the pupils to participate. Alternatively, your school's IT staff may have a way of setting up a discussion forum via specific commercial computer programs such as WebCT (**www.webct.com**), which allows complete control over a discussion forum, but would enable pupils to access it from school as well as home.

USING A NOTICE BOARD FOR LANGUAGE LEARNING

As has been said before, the notice board's main use is that of enabling discussion between a group of individuals. For the language learner, the advantage is that there is enough time to read and translate messages, then to take care in formulating a reply, making notice boards a suitable medium for both beginners and advanced language learners. A teacher's input here can be very important, and is dependent on the level of maturity within the group. Beginners will require more guidance and, initially, it is useful if the teacher accesses all messages to identify potential problems. Once the group is established, codes can be used to help cut down on the teacher's work load. Pupils can, for example, be asked to add '???' to the title of their message if the content requires the teacher's assistance. These opportunities for differentiated

Notice boards

support allow notice boards to be used with groups of varying ability and encourage peer learning. Below are four possible scenarios for the use of notice boards with a group.

Using pre-existing notice boards

In a school context there are limits to the extent to which publicly available notice boards can be exploited because of security issues, but they are worth considering because of the significant benefits to language learning. There are literally hundreds of thousands of notice boards on the Internet and they all give pupils the chance to communicate with native speakers. Unfortunately, the lifetime of notice boards is unpredictable. Notice boards which have not had a contribution for several years may still remain active, while those which see a lot of activity may only last for a few months. All this makes it nearly impossible to provide pupils with a useful list of notice boards to visit. There is no shortage of notice boards, for example entering the words 'Harry Potter' and 'discussion' at **www.yahoo.fr** renders no less than 9,000 results. While not all of these may be relevant, chances are that pupils will find a notice board on almost any topic of their choice in the target language. Using available notice boards will help pupils to get a native speaker's perspective of a topic, or simply encourage them to converse with a 'real person'. Notice boards with a majority of adults participating often render the best results, particularly if the magic words 'I'm learning French at school, and I wondered if anybody could help me' are part of the message – teachers might want to read through the messages on the noticeboard first to gauge the likelihood of success, as well as potential security issues. Short surveys can attract a dozen replies and, if the pupils take care with the message, somebody is likely to take care with an answer, giving the pupil a motivating and successful experience.

Pre-existing notice boards are usually best used as described above – for a one-off, short-term project to obtain information in a school-based language-learning situation. For example, the teacher could find an appropriate notice board, take the class into the IT room, show them how to compose a message (a survey, a request for information on a particular topic) and return one or two weeks later for the replies. These can then be distributed among the entire class. In this way, it is possible to allow pupils to collect answers to their particular question, which will relate to other pupils' questions, forming an overall survey or picture of the chosen topic.

Security remains an issue with open notice boards, and each school will have a different policy regarding the use of the Internet for communicative purposes. In extreme cases, it may be possible for the pupils to give their proposed messages to the teacher, who will enter them under their own user name and then return with the entire class to access the replies later. This would prevent the pupils from entering any potentially harming information into the system, yet would allow them to see the effect of on-line communication and experience the linguistic benefits of obtaining information from a native speaker.

A notice board within one class

A notice board can be of advantage even if there is no native speaker group to communicate with, extending classroom discussion or moving it to a different level. Pupils may, for example, be encouraged to discuss the language-learning process itself in a specific strand, discussing how they learn vocabulary or prepare for examinations, share hints and tips for remembering grammar structures, etc – this is likely largely to be in the mother tongue. This discussion could obviously take place in the classroom, but it is often outside the lesson that pupils come across specific problems they want to discuss. A notice board also allows pupils to come back to older messages and read advice given at an earlier stage of their learning process. In this way, pupils are not only able to retrace their own learning, they can also take responsibility for the group and help one another. Those schools with access to native speakers (Foreign Language Assistant, community links) may find a way to incorporate these native linguists into the notice board, maybe by providing a 'linguistic agony aunt' strand where pupils have the chance to ask questions relating to the target language.

It is possible to discuss topics in the target language within a class, encouraging pupils to communicate with one another and reuse language learned in class. Of course, here only the teacher is likely to offer a highly accurate linguistic model which may not fit in with the teacher's objective for running a project or be feasible in terms of time. Another alternative is to exploit a notice board as the home of a longer-term project. This would allow pupils to display their work within a strand, have it discussed, review it, and produce a piece of work at the end. In this way, a notice board allows a group to keep a long-term project going without spending too much time on it in class, while making the project accessible to pupils both from home and from school, allowing them to upload

Notice boards

information whenever it suits them (rather than having to remember to bring a floppy disk in on the right day). A long-term project using a notice board might work like this:

> **Long-term project using a notice board**
> - A class decides to write a guide to their hometown in the foreign language, making it a project for half a term (six weeks). Between them, they subdivide the information into sports, music, buildings, general facts and the surrounding area, splitting up so that each sub-topic is covered by one group of pupils.
> - The teacher sets up a notice board with a strand for each subtopic, plus a general strand for communication between the groups. This extends the learning process outside the classroom, allowing pupils to access information both from home and from school, as well as creating a 'common ground' for the whole group.
> - Over the next three weeks, the teacher uses the time in lessons to introduce general sentence structures which may be applicable to all subgroups, such as 'In Manchester, there is/are ...', 'Manchester has the biggest/longest/widest ... in the UK', 'there are many opportunities for ... in Manchester', etc.
> - Pupils use these phrases to post ideas relating to their subgroups on the notice board. When pupils continue their work from home, they can post their contributions to the notice board. The teacher also accesses the notice board to keep an eye on the work taking place, as well as providing guidance related to language issues and the distribution of work according to ability within the group. The focus slowly moves from class-based work to independent work outside lessons and pupils without Internet access at home are allowed to use the school computers during lunchtimes.
> - As most notice boards offer the possibility to post attachments, pupils can display pictures or create and post an actual printable version of their part of the guide with Word or other software. As a group, they bring together each individual's contribution and agree on a version they are happy to share with the other subgroups.
> - In weeks four and five a new general strand called 'Presentation' is opened and each group posts their project, commenting on each other's work. Each group responds to any queries which arise to help others understand their specific subtopic, and the teacher intervenes to make

> sure there is an even participation throughout the group. Over these two weeks, the groups edit their work in response to comments from others.
> - In the final week of the project the guide is printed and presented in front of any other classes in the same Year group, who will in turn produce a piece of work on a different topic the following half term.

Of course, in reality, hardly any project goes as smoothly as this. Pupils will feel insecure with the new medium, technical glitches may delay the project, and teachers may find they are too busy to keep a close eye on what is happening in the forum. These problems can be helped by backing up the on-line checking process with questions in class, or by enlisting the help of a few sixth formers or the language assistant.

Using the notice board for discussions with pupils abroad

In principle, working with two groups is similar to working with one – there is still a need for a framework of tasks and support and, with two teachers sharing the responsibility of keeping the forum going, communication is crucial to make sure roles are not duplicated and all aspects of the exchange are covered. When two different native speaker groups participate, the stranding of the notice board might be successfully changed from topic to languages – one strand in each language, plus one for mixed communications and/or help. Pupils access the strand in the target language to post questions to the other group, which the other group answers in their mother tongue, thus creating a model for the language-learning pupils to emulate. In the other strand, the roles are reversed, those who emulate in the first strand now lead by example in their own language.

The teacher has the job of drawing attention to the topic at hand, coaxing reluctant pupils into participating and getting overly enthusiastic spirits to pay more attention to grammar and spelling. Messages openly inviting contributions from specific pupils (*Mark, qu'est-ce que tu penses?*) can help to reawaken the 'dormant' participants. A teacher may choose to play devil's advocate, side with the weakest pupils to help them develop their argument etc, just as in classroom discussions. If there are two members of staff (one from each country), it might be a good idea for each to head the discussion strand which is in their mother tongue, showing their own pupils how to help the foreign pupils with their language learning and to be at hand for questions

Notice boards

which the pupils may not be able to answer. This is not to say, of course, that the teachers will be restricted to their own language – by also working with the pupils as a participant in the foreign language, pupils will get to see their teacher in a different role, i.e. that of the continuous learner, and the teachers may welcome the opportunity to engage in discussions themselves.

In an exchange such as the one described above it will be possible to gather good quality target language material. Also the format may be used successfully to gather target language input for research, such as projects or oral topics. Teachers may want to encourage their pupils to practise discussion-based vocabulary and for the group to get to know each other, before moving on to discussing topics in real time in an oral-communication chat room (see Chapter 5, p53).

Notice boards such as the Yahoo! Groups (**www.groups.yahoo.com**) allow the posting of many other materials besides text, and a good way to get started in a discussion group restricted to the two groups would be for each pupil to upload a little text about themselves (in the mother tongue, the target language or both, according to ability), together with a photo of themselves and possibly even a short sound bite. This helps greatly with one of the disadvantages of notice boards, the fact that it can be difficult to remember who is who, particularly in groups larger than seven or eight. Once pupils have read a message from somebody, they have the chance to refer back to the first message posted by that individual and remind themselves of who they are dealing with. Of course it is vital to respect the school ICT policy in terms of posting pupil details on the Internet and it is crucial that a secure notice board is set up specifically for such an exchange.

Playing out a fantasy role

Similar in essence to the story-writing idea on pp23–25, notice boards offer a 'fantastic' opportunity for language learning seized on by many Internet users – namely a fantasy role-play club. There are literally thousands of on-line role-play clubs on the Internet and, while some are very sophisticated with moving graphics and programmed interventions (called MUDs or MOOs: **www.well.ac.uk/wellclas/moo/moo.htm** or **www.alladin.ac.uk/support/moo/about.html**), many take the form of a simple notice board. On asking around, teachers may find that a large number of pupils are already engaged in such role plays, and many will be keen to try something similar in a foreign language.

INFOTECH
Communicating on-line

The idea of role play consists of a group of players who each assume an identity and live through 'adventures'. These adventures are written by the group, and everybody acts and reacts with one another. Whoever writes the next message continues to spin the story. Messages vary in length according to the writer's wishes, needs or abilities, making this form of writing perfect for differentiated work. Reading what other members have written can prove just as complicated, leaving the learner the choice of using a dictionary or asking for help. On-line role players have developed a coding system of 'ic' (in character) and 'ooc' (out of character) messages to allow them to share and ask for information and, in the language-learning context, these abbreviations may well be used to request clarification on a language-related issue.

Although the amount of language being produced which will be usable in the foreign language classroom will be limited (sooner or later, most role-play clubs drift into fantasy and/or science fiction and the vocabulary related to it), the motivation of spinning a story and 'living' through an adventure in two languages can be enough to have a lasting effect on the language learner, forging links with native speakers and allowing the learner to see that communication can be achieved even on a highly abstract level. (After all, if you can battle a dragon in Spanish, you can ask for two return tickets on the next train to Madrid!) As far as the National Curriculum is concerned, using creativity to cope with unexpected language can hardly be taken further than this sort of role-play situation – solving linguistic problems becomes a necessity, otherwise the storyline becomes inaccessible.

Rather than using the specific notice board features to collaborate on a number of outcomes, here, the storyline is all, and the notice board is merely a convenient method to move the plot along. Talking about somebody else (the fantasy character) may encourage shy pupils to participate more fully and talkative pupils have the chance to create a 'brash' character who can take over situations. This kind of differentiation will happen automatically, as fantasy role-play clubs tend to be self-governing environments.

Notice boards

How to ... make role play work

Role-play clubs will not work for all pupils and are probably best left to volunteers within the class. If there are a number of pupils who are interested in this form of writing, they should first each pick a character and write down a physical description in both languages. These can then be posted, together with the characters' names, on the notice board. Teachers may decide to remain outside the plot, providing linguistic input and monitoring progress.

Once these initial decisions have been reached, what remains is to start an adventure. The beginning can be as simple as the following:

> It is the summer fair in the town of Rigendall and, once more, it is raining. Dara [the teacher's character] is running from cover to cover. She has no money in her pockets, but the food at the fair looks delicious. While she is thinking about what she might eat for tea, a stranger comes up to her and begins to talk.

If there are any practised role players in the group, one of them is likely to immediately assume the role of the 'stranger', starting a conversation. As pupils will wish to use vocabulary far beyond the GCSE specification, you will want to allow them to insert words in the mother tongue where necessary. By encouraging pupils to try and rephrase incorrect sentences, exchanges like *'Hast du meine* sword *gesehen? Nein, ich habe dein Schwert nicht gesehen, tut mir Leid'* are very likely to happen. An actual message from such a role-play club follows in the screen grab opposite.

INFOTECH
Communicating on-line

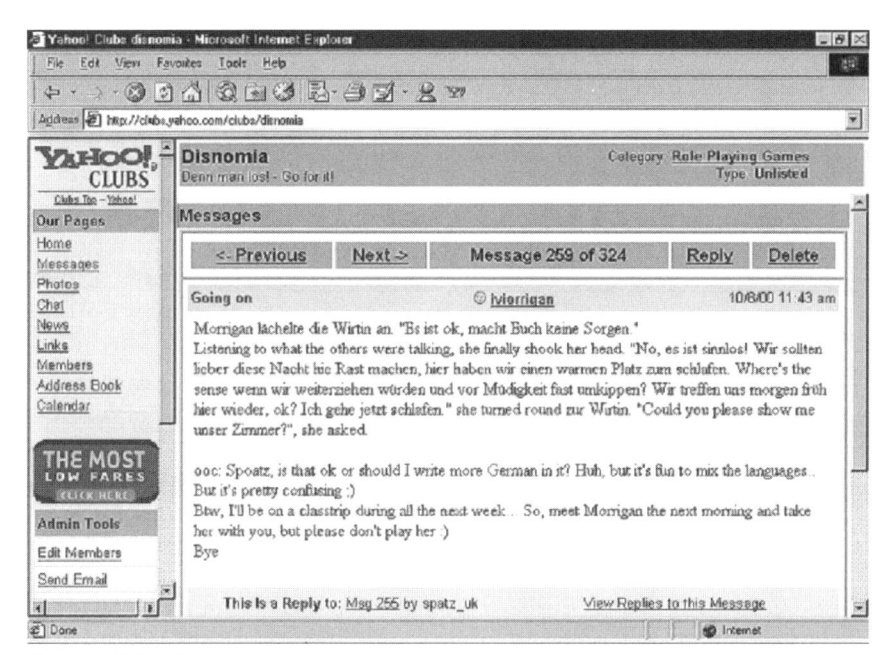

Source: Yahoo!

Not all teachers will feel at ease in a fantasy environment, and each will have to decide whether encouraging pupils to take on an 'alter ego' is desirable. Similarly, some pupils may simply not like the idea of fantasy role play, no matter what language is used – they may think the idea of describing flamboyant battle scenes, campsites at night and treasures to search for childish (or pretend they do). For the more realistic (and/or timid), it is of course also possible to stick to the more straightforward story writing described in the previous chapter. Whichever shape the notice board takes, it will always provide pupils with the opportunity to spin their thoughts or a tale in collaboration with other people, extending vocabulary and group communication skills in the process.

4 Using messaging and chat rooms

In contrast to the communicative possibilities discussed so far in the context of e-mail and notice boards, **synchronous** on-line communication taps into a completely different set of pupil skills. In written synchronous communication, all pupils who are participating in a conversation are actually sitting at their respective computers and whatever they are typing appears almost simultaneously on the screen of the other participant. Rather than placing the emphasis on carefully composed grammar and checked spelling, synchronous communication relies on the strategies of spontaneous communication – thinking on your feet, rephrasing known sentence structures to suit the context, eliciting meaning from the context, and taking risks with vocabulary and sentence structures. A quick glance at the National Curriculum Programme of Study reveals the importance of these skills in language learning, for both written and oral communication:

Pupils should be taught:

- **2d** *how to initiate and develop conversations;*
- **2f** *how to adapt language they already know for different contexts;*
- **2g** *strategies for dealing with the unpredictable;*
- **3b** *how to use context and other clues to interpret meaning.*

The real and immediate contexts within which pupils should be studying MFL are also highlighted under the Breadth of Study:

INFOTECH
Communicating on-line

Using messaging and chat rooms

5d *producing and responding to different types of spoken and written language, including texts produced using ICT;*
5e *using a range of resources, including ICT, for accessing and communicating information;*
5h *using the target language for real purposes.*

Whether communication is via the written word or oral, communicating in this context requires a certain level of spontaneity from the pupils and an ability to express themselves well enough and quickly enough to keep a conversation going. Having to wait for ten minutes for a reply will soon bore even the most enthusiastic language learner, which is why synchronous communication is usually reserved for the more advanced linguist, or needs to be carefully prepared by the teacher and the class. When it all works, however, the immediacy of synchronous communication can be much more motivating than a comparatively slow e-mail exchange. This chapter deals with written communication only, firstly looking at two different types of communication, messaging and chat rooms, then moving on to explore how these media are used to their best effect. For ideas on using audio chat rooms, please see Chapter 5, p53.

MESSAGING

Messaging via the Internet is a one-to-one exchange not that different from text messaging with a mobile phone, which might explain the appeal it has for many pupils. In fact, messaging and e-mailing are the most common forms of on-line language-learning exchange. Messaging facilities are provided by a variety of software programs which can be downloaded from the Internet, most of them free of charge (see 'How to …' box overleaf).

Messages are exchanged by typing and hitting 'Return' whenever a message is finished. It is then displayed to the partner who replies in kind.

The length of a message depends entirely on the author, but messages are often rather short, which tends to confine the use of messaging to more impromptu communication rather than carefully prepared exchanges. At the same time, though, this brevity can be exactly what is needed to motivate those pupils who

INFOTECH
Communicating on-line

Using messaging and chat rooms

may find longer messages more daunting. For teachers trying to get pupils to communicate, messaging offers the focus of one-to-one communication together with the familiarity of the medium (most pupils will be used to either messaging on the Internet or text messaging on their mobile phones). The road is therefore clear for linguistic goals, rather than dealing with unfamiliar media and, in about half an hour on-line, with a pre-prepared list of questions, pupils of most abilities will be able to find out a lot from the partner and later work individually to combine the information into a short profile. This working method allows for differentiation by outcome and makes it easier for weaker pupils to take part in synchronous communication, rather than being overtaken by events in a written chat room, where the conversation might develop so quickly they cannot keep up. In principle, therefore, messaging offers useful opportunities – allowing for exchanges on-line of a manageable length, which still require typed words and thus encourage pupils to pay attention to spelling.

How to ... get started in messaging

Go to the website of the messaging service provider you have chosen. Providers such as Yahoo! Messenger (**http://messenger.yahoo.com**), Microsoft MSN (**http://messenger.msn.co.uk**) and ICQ (**http://web.icq.com**) all offer the same basic service.

Follow the instructions to download the program.

❶ ❷ You will probably be asked to choose a user name and a password – make sure you remember these. When choosing a user name, remember that it will be visible on the Internet, so your pupils should be encouraged to pick a neutral name (suggestions made by providers usually combine a colour and a number, such as 'blue1468', or randomly combined words, such as 'woodbeaver45', etc – doing this with a dictionary in the target language can actually be very entertaining for the pupils).

❸ When the program is installed it will, in all likelihood, create a shortcut (an icon on the desktop) for future access. If not, you will find it again by clicking on the 'Start' button at the bottom left and looking under 'Programs'.

❹ If you know somebody else who is using the same program and you know their user name, you can search for them and add them to your 'buddy list', which will show you how many of the other users you know are on-line at any one time (see opposite).

Messaging also holds great motivational potential, precisely because pupils are so familiar with the medium. For language-learning purposes, messaging can be seen as a supporting medium rather than the sole means of on-line communication. For two learners engaged in a functioning e-mail exchange (see Chapter 2), messaging back and forth while surfing the Web will cement the relationship and give a bit of 'light relief' from more in-depth e-mails. For a pupil who has a standing Internet connection, seeing that the e-mail partner is on-line might inspire a quick message asking about an item of vocabulary or turn of phrase in his or her homework, further encouraging independent learning.

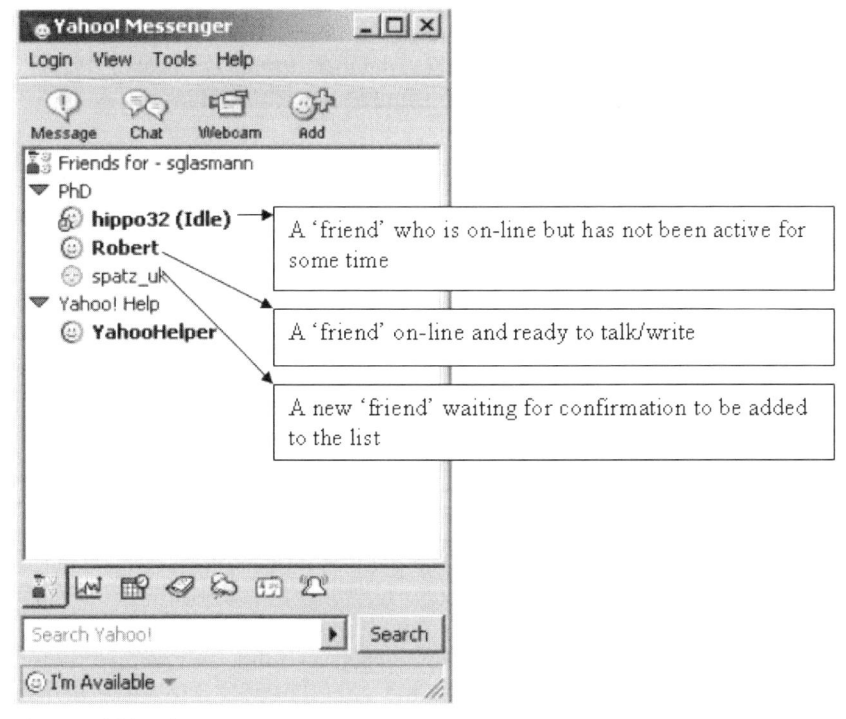

[Yahoo! Messenger screenshot showing:
- hippo32 (Idle) → A 'friend' who is on-line but has not been active for some time
- Robert → A 'friend' on-line and ready to talk/write
- spatz_uk / YahooHelper → A new 'friend' waiting for confirmation to be added to the list]

Source: Yahoo!

There are some practical limitations to messaging to consider, however.

- Be aware that some messaging programs might only display single messages in chronological order, which may not be very user friendly. If only

individual messages are sent back and forth, a question may be long forgotten by the time the answer arrives. Here notice boards may have an advantage, as it is possible to display messages in conversation 'strands', adding the latest one to the end.
- As with text messaging on mobile phones, a similar approach to spelling and shortened words has become apparent in on-line messaging, making it difficult to reap linguistic benefits from the exchange.
- Most people do not message exclusively while they are on-line – they either message with several people at the same time, juggling messages as they come in, or they message while they do some other work – surfing the Internet, etc. This shift in concentration can mean that exchanges become nearly meaningless and frequently degenerate to the lowest level of 'Sorry?', 'What?', 'My turn or urs?', 'Dunno', 'Hmm', 'Hmm ...', and so on.

Because messaging is more of a complementary facility than a focus for communication, it can be used very successfully by pupils outside the classroom. However to practise true spontaneous on-line writing, chat rooms are a more appropriate medium.

CHAT ROOMS

Where messaging functions one-to-one, chat rooms are open to a (theoretically) unlimited number of people, making it therefore the first medium discussed in this book that enables a meeting of a group on-line in real time. Similar to messaging, 'entering' a chat room opens a new window on the computer. The list of people present is displayed on one side and there is a small section at the bottom of the window which enables the pupil to type in messages and check them before sending them by hitting 'Return'. A lot of sites host their own chat rooms; there are, however, also chat programs whose sole purpose is to give access to a vast number of chat rooms, such as mIRC (**www.mirc.com**). Programs such as mIRC are shareware, meaning that after a free trial period, users will have to buy a licence to continue using the program.

For language-learning purposes, chat rooms allow for a written discussion between several people, producing an environment where pupils of different abilities can work together, share knowledge and experiences, and practise explaining language points without having to rely on one partner alone. Group dynamics are, of course, an issue in a chat room. Some weaker pupils may be reassured by being allowed just to read what other users are typing, without having to actively produce language themselves, and they may relish the opportunity of being exposed to language without any pressures. Others might prefer a smaller environment as they feel 'useless' not being able to communicate themselves. Maintaining the balance can be difficult – see 'Mediating a chat room' on p52.

Practicalities of using a chat room

Setting up a chat room is getting easier all the time – in fact, every newly founded Yahoo! Group automatically includes one, which has one distinct advantage: if the Yahoo! Group has been labelled as 'private', access to the chat room is automatically restricted (see Chapters 3 and 5 for more information on Yahoo! Groups). Use of a chat room creates a real opportunity for discussion on-line. Some chat rooms already integrate audio and/or video, which are explored in Chapter 5, but as not all of them do, the opportunities for written discussion are primarily discussed here.

With chat rooms being a synchronous form of communication, all on-line exchanges between groups in different countries need to be timed carefully – with time differences between one hour (Europe) and eight or nine hours (Asia), this can create serious problems when it comes to time-tabling. As all schools are likely to have different time-tables, there is, unfortunately, no general remedy for this problem. Lunch times, after school clubs, access from home, a change in the time-table, or indeed pure luck might all be possible answers, depending on individual schools.

One of the advantages of chat rooms is that communication can be stored for future reference. By highlighting the text, it can be copied and pasted into a Word or text document. This technique allows pupils to store not only those bits of the conversation they want to work with later, but also words they don't understand (but don't want to interrupt the flow of communication to ask about), as well as storing whole chunks of text as proof of the communication for the teacher, should the exchange happen out of school time.

Using messaging and chat rooms

Security issues

As with notice boards, chat rooms are in principle accessible to everyone, unless they are closed, i.e. created as a private chat room. For this reason, many school networks have a 'firewall' which will automatically block access to chat rooms, as well as to websites or e-mail messages containing inappropriate language. Again, talking to the IT staff may literally open doors – once a reputable chat room has been found, or a private chat room created, it will be possible to allow access to the site. Chat rooms are an excellent way to gain access to native speakers, explore cultural communication and get input in the foreign language that can easily be stored, retrieved and used later – the effort involved is, therefore, really worthwhile.

Open chat rooms can be accessed by anybody and, although many of those created specifically for children are monitored, the truth is that it is very difficult to know exactly who is in the chat room at any one time. Pupils over the age of 18, especially those savvy in the world of chatting, might want to check out the thousands of multilingual chat rooms on-line from home in their own time, but for the younger ones it is advisable to create a chat room especially for their language-learning exchange, and use the suggestions made in the Conclusion of this book to find a partner class to engage with.

Linguistic conventions

Due to the nature of synchronous communication, chat room users frequently do not type out full words, using 'brb' for 'be right back' and 'lol' for 'laughing out loud', for example. Many of these English abbreviations have penetrated the international on-line community, which can be frustrating when you want your pupils to focus on the target language. One way around this is to encourage pupils to create their own abbreviations, or to make the explanation of 'what means what' the topic of the conversation for a while.

Emoticons, a combination of letters, punctuation and numbers (see below), are another way to quickly state a frame of mind, and most of them are read by tilting the head to the left by 90°. Emoticons can be a fun way to work on pupils' expressive language skills at the same time as speeding up their on-line communication.

Using messaging and chat rooms

101 sind online | Wer ist online?	Infoladen A - Z | Hilfe | Suche Login
Chat | Anleitung | Chatiquette | Emoticons | Hilfe	chat

Kindernetz-Chat
Emoticons und Chat-Kürzel für Chat-Profis

Emoticons

:-)	erfreutes, fröhliches Lachen
:-D	schallendes Lachen
;-)	augenzwinkerndes Lachen
:-(	trauriges, unglückliches Gesicht
:-*	freundschaftlicher Kuss
:-o	Erstaunen
:-p	Zunge rausstrecken *bäh*
:-x	Schweigen, Ich sag es nicht weiter

© SWR Kindernetz
Source: www.kindernetz.de/quasselbude/emoticons/index.html

After looking at some existing emoticons, pupils can be given an 'emoticon quiz' (see below) which requires them to link emoticons to adjectives, or even invent them.

Here are a few emoticons. Can you invent more to match the words?

:-)	I am happy.	*Estoy feliz.*
___	I am very happy.	*Estoy muy contento.*
:-O	I am surprised.	*Estoy sorprendido.*
___	I am sad.	*Estoy triste.*
___	I am angry.	*Estoy enfadado.*
___	I am scared.	*Estoy asustado.*
___	I am tired.	*Estoy cansado.*
___	I am bored.	*Estoy aburrido.*

INFO**T**eCH
Communicating on-line

Using messaging and chat rooms

APPROACHES TO LANGUAGE LEARNING USING A CHAT ROOM

Below are three examples of how groups from different countries might successfully use a chat room for language-learning purposes. These examples assume that a link with a foreign school has already been established. For guidance on how to set up a link, see the Conclusion. For ideas on how to deal with different class sizes and abilities, please refer to Chapter 5.

Example 1: Supporting a class-to-class exchange with a school abroad

A Year 9 class is preparing for a French exchange. As part of the partner schools' joint preparations, their teachers create an on-line chat room where pupils can meet in real time to get to know each other (depending on the size of the classes, several chat rooms may have to be created – the number of pupils who can efficiently work together on-line varies greatly and will need to be worked out individually).

Initially, each pupil receives the name of a partner, together with an e-mail address where the partner can be contacted. The pupils then have one or two weeks to make the first contact via e-mail and find out general information about the partner – age, hobbies, pets, etc.

After the initial contact, both classes devise a list of questions in the target language, asking the other group about their opinions. These questions can range from opinions about school subjects to music, films or actors, to more complicated issues such as the environment, depending on the pupils' ability.

Having prepared the questions, the UK group also prepares their own answers (in French) to these questions. These answers are not shown to the French group, but they are used to compare the language with what the French group writes and are modified once the answers from the French group have been received, according to new structures and new vocabulary encountered. Likewise, the French group would do the same activity, but working in English.

To enable language learning, all pupils agree to type proper words rather than use abbreviations and, in order to encourage discussion, both groups practise discussion vocabulary such as the following in the target language. The list is obviously endless, determined only by the pupils' ability.

Using messaging and chat rooms

Français	Deutsch	Español
Qu'est-ce que tu penses?	Was denkst du?	¿Tú que piensas?
Et toi?	Und du?	¿Y tu?
Moi aussi.	Ich auch.	Yo también.
J'ai le même problème.	Ich habe das gleiche Problem.	Tengo el mismo problema.
Ce n'est pas vrai!	Das ist nicht wahr!	¡Eso no es verdad!
C'est un peu fort.	Das ist ein bisschen stark!	¡Es un poco fuerte!
Que dire!	Was soll ich dazu sagen!	Que digo yo!
Je sais ce que je dis.	Ich weiß, was ich sage.	Sé lo que digo. Se de lo que estoy hablando.
C'est facile à dire.	Das ist leicht gesagt.	Es fácil decirlo.
Je crois que nous sommes d'accord.	Ich glaube, wir sind uns einig.	Creo que estamos de acuerdo.
Je n'y connais rien.	Davon verstehe ich nichts.	No se nada sobre esto.
C'est vrai ou pas?	Stimmt das oder nicht?	¿Es correcto o no?
C'est exact.	Das ist richtig.	Es asi. Está bien.

The two groups arrange to meet on-line in the chat room at a certain time, where the English group will post their questions in French and receive answers in the same language, and vice versa. In this way, the emphasis is still placed on understanding the foreign language, rather than producing it – the English pupils will find it easy to respond in English to the questions the French group poses in English, but may have to concentrate harder to understand the French answers to their own questions, which is where their preparation, answering the questions in French themselves, will help (see above). To make sure the conversation is available for future use, the pupils copy and paste the exchange

INFOTECH
Communicating on-line

Using messaging and chat rooms

into a Word or text document and save it as a document which can be manipulated or printed. A subsequent whole-class discussion in English on some of the exchanges can identify both linguistic and technical challenges, as well as tie what has happened in the chat room to what is happening in the classroom. By combining several such shorter exchanges, pupils can build up a portfolio of information, or use the information from one particular exchange to create an information booklet, manipulating electronic text and inserting pictures, or indeed preparing a talk (with or without the aid of technical programs such as PowerPoint), to introduce the topic to a parallel class. After the official project period finishes, the chat room can remain accessible to the pupils should they wish to continue the on-line exchanges with a group of pupils or their individual partners.

Example 2: Topical discussion

Whereas Example 1 was aimed at getting to know the other group better, the topical discussion described here is operating on a higher level, taking into account different areas of experience. A Year 11 class is preparing for the oral examination and would like to gain insight into problems and issues related to German life and culture. The English pupils prepare questions in German they would like to have answered but, in contrast to the exchange described above, they also prepare further questions, seeking opinions, attitudes and comparisons, such as:

Wie findest du das?

Was hältst du davon?

Stört dich das?

Bist du damit zufrieden?

Denken alle Leute so wie du?

Ist das nicht eigennützig/dumm/besser?

The groups decide on recycling for their first topic. Starting off with a simple question such as *Recycelst du?* or *Was recycelst du?* they get the ball rolling. Whenever they have problems they either switch to English to receive help from the German pupils or they ask their teacher – perhaps using a private communication facility. Many chat rooms have a private communication function, which can usually be started by right-clicking on a username from the list on the side. If the program supports private conversations, the option for 'private chat' or 'message this user' or similar should appear. This facility allows pupils to communicate with their teacher without anyone noticing – although it also works the other way round and pupils might be covertly chatting to one another outside the chat room without the teacher noticing. Teachers should be aware of this feature and be vigilant. Again, the conversation is saved for future reference by copying and pasting. Some programs allow for saving a chat room conversation for several days without copy and paste – an option worth exploring (usually found under 'safety issues' listed by the respective providers).

Back in the classroom the discussion can be evaluated and turned into phrases reflecting the differences between the recycling system in England and Germany, and incorporated into GCSE oral questions, a writing frame for coursework, etc. Any expressions used by the German pupils which were misunderstood are explained and noted down to make future conversations easier. A new topic can then be prepared (such as the school system, food, etc), or the chat room can simply be left open to the pupils for individual future use. While communication happens largely in the target language, it is likely that more complicated issues will still be discussed in English, allowing the German pupils (who generally have a higher command of the target language) to learn in the process as well. If a more structured switch of languages is desired, it might be possible to create two different types of chat room with 'language flags', one German, one English, allowing pupils to switch from one to the other to follow or participate in discussions. Alternatively, the language focus in a longer exchange might change from topic to topic, or each group might use their respective mother tongue to capture the full width and breadth of expressions. This will depend on motivation, linguistic ability and intended outcomes.

Example 3: From asynchronous notice board to synchronous chat room

Both notice boards and chat rooms facilitate discussion on-line and, in carefully preparing the transition from using a notice board to using a chat room, the pupil is also prepared for the more spontaneous exchange that occurs in chat rooms. For example, if the first topic of the exchange for the asynchronous stage is food, pupils from both groups post their assumptions about food in the other country on the notice board – in the target language if they can. The pupils then comment on the notices and post their replies – e.g. not all British people eat bacon and eggs for breakfast, nor does the whole of France live on *croissants*. Whenever pupils want to use an expression they don't know (such as 'that's not true', 'why do you think that?', 'I always thought …' etc), they ask for a translation and post it under a specific strand on the notice board. After the project is finished, the pupils draw these expressions together to create a phrase book for their next, more spontaneous discussion, which will happen in the chat room. Once they have proven to themselves that they can exchange comments and opinions with a native speaker, meeting the other group in 'real time' will be a natural next step. With newly learnt discussion phrases under their belt, a new topic to discuss at the synchronous stage and a teacher on hand in case of emergencies, the synchronous on-line exchange is likely to run much more smoothly.

MEDIATING A CHAT ROOM

As mentioned above, having a large number of participants in an on-line discussion can become problematic – several 'hellos', and 'goodbyes', may lie between a question and its answer, contributions might go unnoticed, etc. To minimise this, it is possible to mediate a chat room by controlling who is allowed to 'speak' (i.e. type). Mediation is best introduced to a chat room by a teacher, although pupils may appoint their own mediator at a later date. One of the simplest forms of mediation is that pupils are required to type in a question mark and hit 'Return' to indicate that they would like to speak. The mediator then types in the name of whoever's turn it is, thus shaping the conversation. This also allows the mediator to elicit answers from shyer participants, by asking a pupil a direct question before picking the next contribution. In oral chat rooms mediation is vital, as in many programs anybody who speaks automatically blocks any others and the conversation can risk being dominated by a few speakers. For this reason, oral chat rooms such as PalTalk (www.paltalk.com) have a 'raised hand' symbol to indicate the wish to speak. In the next chapter there is more on this issue.

5 Integrating the four skills

So far, the focus of this book has been on the written word for purposes of on-line communication, and for a good reason. Tried and tested, e-mail, notice boards and even written chat rooms have been around for years and the learning opportunities they represent have been the focus of studies, articles and classroom practice. However, particularly in language learning, on-line communication has until recently neglected listening and speaking. Today, contact with native speakers is not restricted to writing but allows pupils to practise speaking in the target language, to focus on their pronunciation and to hone their listening comprehension skills. However, there is a catch – organising audio on-line exchanges is not easy, and it is not only the pupils who will need to think on their feet! This final chapter will look at ideas for exploring opportunities for the integration of the spoken word.

The possibility of using the Internet to create audio links with a partner school sounds like a solution to many schools' problems regarding authentic contact, especially those without access to native speakers. Working with an on-line partner via an audio link covers many of the Programme of Study requirements:

Pupils should be taught how to:

- **2a** *listen carefully for gist and detail;*
- **2b** *correct pronunciation and intonation;*
- **2c** *ask and answer questions;*
- **2d** *initiate and develop conversations;*
- **2e** *vary the target language to suit context, audience and purpose.*

Integrating the four skills

The Breadth of Study also suggests pupils should learn through:

5d producing and responding to different types of spoken and written language;

5g listening, reading or viewing for personal interest and enjoyment, as well as for information;

5h using the target language for real purposes.

There are also, of course, the obvious benefits for cultural knowledge and understanding of working in an authentic environment, as highlighted in the Programme of Study.

While – in theory – it is true that virtually anything is possible, in reality there are quite a number of practical considerations to take into account when it comes to creating opportunities for audio communication. More often than not, audio and/or video links will be used to support written exchanges, rather than as a one-off activity. Many of the ideas described here therefore, presume that some contact between the learners already exists and this chapter suggests how to exploit Internet-based services for the integration of all four skills, rather than concentrating on the incorporation of listening and speaking only.

MAKING AUDIO LINKS WORK

Many on-line communities already feature facilities for audio and even video communication. Yahoo! Groups, for example, include a chat room which offers spoken communication. Many messaging programmes, such as Yahoo! Messenger, also include an audio option for one-to-one communication. To make this type of on-line work available for entire classes can be quite tricky from a technical as well as an organisational point of view – having all 30 pupils access the same site not only slows down the system, but all 30 pupils using an audio facility creates a substantial noise in the classroom, always provided there are 30 sets of computers and headphones in the first place! This form of exchange, therefore, needs careful preparation, as bad execution of a plan can be detrimental to the pupils' learning – it will be difficult to control, and the pupils themselves will have problems maintaining concentration for more than a few minutes at a time. However, there are a number of ways around these problems.

If only one computer is available, the audio output can be put on loudspeaker, allowing pupils to take turns with the daunting task of communicating, with the other pupils supporting and listening. This option is possible with both audio messaging and chatrooms. Pupils whose turn it is to communicate should be warned in advance and perhaps given the chance to prepare phrases and vocabulary with the teacher and/or their peers. If the whole class helps to prepare the communication that will take place, it will be easier to remain focused even though the onus of activity may be placed on a select few. Having had an input in the creation of questions, pupils can be encouraged to listen for answers, write down unknown vocabulary, or even be on call for the communicating pupil, forming a supportive 'task force'. In a class of 30, two pupils might be chosen to share the communication, three to keep an eye on the written conversation on-screen, five on 'dictionary call', looking up words when needed to keep the conversation flowing, the rest noting down what is being said. By rotating these tasks, pupils are practising all four skills, and are also summarising, taking notes and carrying out dictionary work.

A number of other viable approaches are described in the following pages.

Using audio with messaging

Once you and your pupils are accustomed to the written form of messaging, as explained in Chapter 3, you may wish to start exploiting the audio facility. On p42, we explain how to install a messaging program, create a user name and create a list of 'friends'.

The instructions in the 'How to …' box below will help you to maximise lesson time for language learning and avoid logistical problems when extending the messaging facility to include an audio option.

Integrating the four skills

How to ... get a full class registered on audio messaging

❶ Pre-install the required messaging program on all the machines to be used for the exchange. It may be possible to install all machines at the same time. For audio links, each machine will need sound capability (i.e. soundcard) and a microphone and headphones. You will need to liase with IT staff to find out if this is possible and in line with school policy.

❷ Prepare a seating plan so you know which pupil is registered on which machine (the program will remember the next time the pupils log on), otherwise you will need to get everybody to re-register every time.

❸ Ask the pupils to create a user name (see Chapter 3) and a password and write them on two pieces of paper, once for themselves, once for you.

❹ Take the class to the computer room, where each pupil registers on one machine with their user name and password.

❺ If a user name has already been registered by someone else, remember to make note of the new user name chosen.

❻ Exchange your list of user names with the partner teacher – it is advisable to add a few notes to indicate which are keen and which are the less able pupils. Decide on suitable pairings.

❼ You can either access each pupil's computer individually and add the partner's name to their list of 'friends', or you can hand out user names on slips of paper and ask pupils to do it themselves (how to 'add a friend' will depend on which program you are using – please read the provider's guidelines for further advice).

If there is an uneven number of pupils, the more able pupils (and/or those experienced in messaging) might be able to cope with having more than one partner. Alternatively, pupils might take turns to work with one partner, using their off-line time to prepare questions and information.

INFO TECH
Communicating on-line

Using audio with chat rooms

One-to-one 'audio stations' as a carousel activity

Another way to integrate use of audio in a chat room – or messaging – activity is to set up a variety of tasks in the computer room, only one of which involves synchronous communication. In the computer room, a small group of computers are set up for an audio chat-room link, and the pupils take it in turns to work at these audio stations, having prepared phrases and questions in advance, supported by a list of vocabulary they might expect to hear in the foreign pupils' answers. Pupils tend to require immediate attention with this type of work and teachers will find it much easier to cope if only a small number of pupils are engaged in it at any one point. There are clearly logistical challenges in organising who will be talking to whom at what point, so one approach is to set up just one user name which can be used by all the pupils in the group. A pupil can then sit down at his or her allocated slot with his or her partner, pick up the headphones, and get started. If working out a bilateral timetable seems too time-consuming, random pupils could use the computer on a five-minute slot rota where pupils have time to find out as much as they can about whoever is at the other end. If the staff themselves are audio-linked, this helps even more as they can discuss problems and changes as they occur during the lesson and can better help pupils, while making it possible to co-ordinate partner changes far more effectively.

Audio chat rooms – the group approach

Another approach which avoids complicated changeovers is the use of an audio chat room (such as Yahoo! Groups and their audio integrated facility), again using a limited number of suitably equipped computers. Pupils need to log on to the discussion group on a computer, click on 'chat room' and engage in oral discussion. Pupils take turns at the computer so that everyone has a chance to to participate. Again, if you prefer to avoid drawing up a bilateral timetable for individuals, you can organise a fixed rotation, with a new group of three or so pupils getting into the chat room every fifteen minutes (making for a total of six pupils in the chat room, three from each country). By making sure the pupils have a set of questions to ask, the comparatively short time can be used efficiently.

Integrating the four skills

APPROACHES TO LANGUAGE LEARNING THROUGH AUDIO COMMUNICATION

There are a number of forms audio communication can take, which include:

- guided tasks (see the example below);
- exchange of questions in advance, so answers can be prepared;
- semi-prepared discussion on an issue;
- role-play transactions, e.g. booking a cinema ticket;
- imaginative role plays – story telling, interviewing famous people, etc.

Communicating via audio over the Internet is very similar to a telephone conversation, in that pupils may feel unprepared and exposed. It can therefore be helpful to start off a partnership in a written format, e.g. via e-mail. Pupils can get to know each other and build up a relationship before they engage in the audio exchange. Likewise you can then build up pupils' confidence through a progression of audio-based activities, starting with structured and prepared activities before moving to the less structured and/or more imaginative, such as those in the list above. Before practising role plays, for example, pupils might work on a guided task, such as the one below.

> **Guided task**
>
> Describe your family. Say where your parents work, whether you've got any brothers or sisters, how you get on with them. Describe the looks and character of two family members. Ask your partner about his or her family and make sure you take notes while you are talking. Check up on all information and vocabulary you are not clear about (such as jobs and spellings). After you have logged off, write a description of your partner's family in the target language and e-mail it to him or her, asking whether you got everything right.

It is this sense of authenticity that will help pupils maintain motivation and it will develop their awareness of how they are learning.

Once pupils are happy with this form of exchange, an actual role play may be the next step. Although it is not necessary to follow the exact layout of, say, a GCSE role-play, many pupils might welcome the chance to practise with their

INFOTECH
Communicating on-line

partner. Others will prefer to use the situations given in role plays as guidance only, to the extreme of being given only a title (e.g. 'At the restaurant') and making up their own exchange, ranging from reserving a table to complaining about food. As it becomes less and less structured, this form of activity bridges the gap between strict framework and complete creativity, allowing pupils to gain in confidence in tandem with gaining in ability.

SUPPORTING AN AUDIO EXCHANGE – HOW TO TALK

By briefing the class about the likely level of their partners' language skills, pupils can be guided in pitching their answers in the mother tongue at a level appropriate to the partner school's level of English, which increases their awareness of their own language. One way of doing this is for pupils to prepare by completing a self-evaluation form, possibly in consultation with a class mate (see p60).

After working with a partner for some time, pupils will be able to give each other feedback on pronunciation and mistakes they make in the foreign language. This information can be formalised into a log of their exchange, focusing on ideas for a way forward, which will encourage them to see the entire exchange as one large learning experience, rather than a number of tasks they have to complete because they were told to. A check list for this feedback may look like the one set out on p61.

ANTICIPATING PROBLEMS WITH SPOKEN ON-LINE COMMUNICATION IN SCHOOLS

On top of any problems which you may need to overcome initially with regard to the school firewall and access to chat rooms (see p45), the teacher must make sure that pupils have the appropriate equipment for audio communication – a headset incorporating headphones and microphone. Such equipment controls the noise level in the classroom and aids clarity of communication. A similar set-up is also required at the partner school, of course! The teacher should also bear in mind that the quality of the transmission can be dependent on a number of things, ranging from the capacity of the school's Internet connection to the

Integrating the four skills

number of people on-line at any one time. At certain times the Internet can get very busy, and when this happens audio links experience a 'lag'. This lag can also occur in written communication, creating difficulties for synchronous conversations. It is, however, more disruptive in audio exchanges where a speaker might break up and re-connect seconds later, either continuing the sentence or leaving a gap of several seconds. Time differences already discussed in Chapter 4 also apply here.

Name: _____

Date: _____ **Form/Group:** _____

I think my pronunciation of English is:
- ☐ clear,
- ☐ clear if I pay attention,
- ☐ possibly difficult to understand for my partner.

I often say words and phrases like (e.g. 'innit?' 'do you know what I mean?'):
_____
_____

I usually speak very fast/fast/slowly/very slowly (delete as appropriate).

I mumble   ☐ yes   ☐ no

When talking to my partner, I will make sure I ...
_____
_____

INFO TECH
Communicating on-line

Integrating the four skills

Name:

Date: **Form/Group:**

My partner says he/she :

☐ can always understand my pronunciation,
☐ can mostly understand my pronunciation,
☐ has difficulty understanding my pronunciation.

I think I did well when I …

These are some of the words I've learnt:

I would like to do some more work on …

My partner says he/she would like help with …

We've decided our next project is going to be …

INFOTECH
Communicating on-line

Integrating the four skills

There are certain 'tricks' to help to make the best of the time on-line:

- afternoon time in Britain means the start of the workday in the USA, which usually slows the Internet down – sticking to morning lessons not only helps with the Internet, but usually also makes for 'perkier' pupils;
- if your school cannot deal with the full class on-line, group pupils together to share, or have only a small number of on-line groups, with other groups completing support work, or other work;
- like any other IT-based lesson, think of what to do when the system crashes, the Internet is down or pupils haven't done the preparatory work – a back-up plan is as valid here as for any other time in the classroom.

MAKING VIDEO LINKS WORK

Whereas audio links require each computer to have individual headphones and microphones, a video link for a class-to-class exchange demands that each computer has its own small Web camera fixed on the monitor. Unfortunately, few schools will be able to accommodate an entire class with a video link at any one time, more likely developing a strategy similar to the 'audio stations' described on p57, allowing a few pupils at a time access to the camera. Another strategy is to project the pictures received from one computer via a data projector onto a wall or screen, so that they can be shared by the whole class, with the pupils taking turns to take 'centre stage' in front of the whole class.

Although there have been many advancements in the area of video links over the last few years, the more affordable technology cannot be compared with the live video coverage we experience from the world of television. To enable video conferencing, each computer being used must be equipped with a Web Cam and have the relevant software installed. Further software is needed depending on which program is to be used for video conferencing – Yahoo! Messenger and Yahoo! Groups include the option to view somebody else's Web Cam, other programs, such as iVisit (**www.ivisit.com**) or PalTalk (**www.paltalk.com**) also have video options. It should be noted that video links on a computer are prone to the same sort of problems as audio communication, such as time lag and fragile connections. Most video links do not transmit continuously – instead the camera updates the picture it sees every few seconds. Even the better cameras do not allow for more than a few frames per second. As a result, what the person at the other end sees can seem rather stilted, like a badly-drawn

INFOTECH
Communicating on-line

cartoon where the individual drawings do not quite fit together. However, with increasing bandwidths on broadband Internet picture quality should continue to improve. Video links are frequently an additional feature to existing audio and/or written communication links, and it is worth noting here that, while every pupil is capable of functioning in everyday life using eyes and ears at the same time, the concentration required to maintain a conversation on a visual, aural, oral and typewritten level can be immense, particularly if more than two people communicate with each other at any one time and in the target language, too. On the other hand, for those pupils who are at their best when learning visually, a video link can be just the thing to get them going. They can speak to a real person rather than listen to disembodied language. In addition, they can make all sorts of interesting cultural observations by seeing images of, for example, what is going on in the classroom. With a very fast Internet connection and good quality equipment and technology, it may even be possible to use lip movement as an aid to linguistic understanding. What follows below are ideas to get pupils involved in using a video link, without placing too many or too complicated demands on the pupil. Creating an on-line learning environment for a group of pupils can be a fantastic way to explore all the options the Internet and on-line communication have to offer.

Step one: Introducing the classes to one another

After an appropriate videolink software has been chosen in collaboration with IT staff and technical support, both classes prepare a presentation, including a short introduction from each pupil. These may stretch over several lessons, or form the first complete session, depending on the pupils' ability to concentrate for longer stretches of time. The camera – an ordinary Internet camera will suffice – may move around (operated by a teacher or a designated 'camera pupil') in order to capture the whole class, groups of friends or individuals. This method will require a bit more preparation from both ends. The 'presenting' class will need to practise their introductions and possible changes of the camera position, while the receiving class will need to find a way to gather as many of the class members around the computer as possible – a data projector will be helpful here, if available – making sure the audio link can be heard by everybody via speakers. By giving the whole class the opportunity to present themselves, teachers can gain a good idea of the extent to which pupils will be able to use the medium when the exchange continues on a more individual level.

Integrating the four skills

Step two: Using the video link for still pictures

It is possible to work within the constraints imposed by the limited quality of video transmission by using the link to transmit still pictures. For example, pupils can bring in photos or pictures to show to the partner by holding them up to the camera. When describing the last family holiday, a few photos from the beach are an excellent stimulus for communication. Not only can pupils see what the listener looks like, but the activity develops their ability to talk to prompts, providing good practice for GCSE oral examinations. Used in this manner, a slow connection will not matter too much, which makes this method accessible for any school that has access to a camera. While the emphasis is still on the spoken word, the pictures supply an authentic cultural input, stimulating communication and possibly questions from the learning partner. Of course, this approach can even be used without a video link at all – by simply e-mailing the photos in advance or by using file-sharing software such as within Microsoft Netmeeting (**www.microsoft.com/windows/netmeeting**), so that the pupils have them to hand.

Step three: Finding an audio/video chat room

Older pupils may want to work independently on their skills of spontaneous discussion and access one of the many audio/video chat rooms on the Internet. Programs such as PalTalk (**www.paltalk.com**) offer a wide variety of chat rooms where turning the video on is optional, and which range in topic and language to incorporate almost any need – for example, at the time of writing the list of Hispanic and Portuguese chat rooms numbers 87 (see opposite).

Spontaneous on-line discussion is, however, very unpredictable – pupils may go on-line one week and find seven other users engaged in a lively, fruitful discussion, only to return a week later to a completely empty chat room.

All security issues already mentioned apply in an audio chat room, pupils should be reminded not to give away their contact details and be wary of other users asking personal questions. Due to the nature of open chat rooms, this method will mainly be suitable for students over 18, but younger pupils can still practise their language skills in a written or audio chat room set up specifically for them – see step 4 below for details.

INFOTECH
Communicating on-line

Integrating the four skills

R.	V.	L.	By Language: Spanish & Portuguese - Group List	#
G			Hable Espanol con Camaras y Fotos (Tom El L...	34
G	🎤		O Minho Portugal	25
G	🎤		Tengo Ganas de Ti ...!!!	24
G	🎤		RincOncit0 De L0s Madurit0s	18
G	🎤		@**PhiLLy In ThE HoUsE**@	15
G	🎤		@@@ Europalive-Portuguesa @@@	15
G	🎤		@@Portugal Norte Sul@@	14
G	🎤		<*>No a la guerra entre USA e IRAK<*>	12
G	🎤		mundo nuevo vida nueva	12
G	🎤		Musica Latina 24 Hrs con Sugar_Boy & Y2k0...	9
G	🎤		@volvamos a la senda antigua@ en vivo@	9
G	🎤		@<---(De MeXico al mundo)--->@	9
G	🎤		Fafe Portugal	7
G	🎤		Sala Bonita	7
G			Chicas Buscan Chicos	4
G	🎤		Oo0 MaTaDoR_SpAiN Oo0	4
G	🎤	🔒	Solas y conversando	3
G	🎤		Um Bom Negocio, Seguro & Rentavel	2
G	🎤		Radio 103.5 FM - Santa Cruz - Argentina	2
G	🎤		Trivadid y los Destrerrados	2
G			Busco una mujer atrevida con Camara	2
G	🎤		Pastor Russell - Dialogo y Analisis	2
G	🎤		@@ Ritimo da balada @@ dj mix brasil @@	2
G	🎤	🔒	Te hecho de menos	2
G	🎤		Karaoke Pa Ti	1
G	🎤		Grupo Electronico Biblico	1
G	🎤		@@@ Central das Amizades @@@	1
G	🎤		Comacates de Venezuela	1

Double-click a Group Item to Join

Source: www.paltalk.com

Step four: Creating an on-line learning environment

Creating a tailor made on-line learning environment is one way to incorporate all skills, tasks and ideas laid out in this book so far, and it is easier than it seems. Although PalTalk does offer the creation of a free chat room, having exclusive (and therefore safe) use of one requires a fee – check the website for current details regarding what is and is not possible.

INFOTECH

Communicating on-line

Integrating the four skills

Creating a Yahoo! Group, as discussed in Chapter 3, will give pupils access to a notice board, a written chat room with an audio link, the possibility of storing photos and files, and even a calendar to remind pupils of forthcoming holidays and/or trips that may influence the on-line exchange – in short, an on-line learning environment that is just waiting to be explored and utilised to its full potential. If the Yahoo! Group has been registered unlisted, the whole environment is completely safe with none of the stored data accessible to outsiders, and the chat rooms impenetrable to people not specifically invited to join. If a Yahoo! Group has already been set up for its notice board, then nothing further needs to be done – the chat room is an automatic feature and the audio function an option which can be enabled and disabled at will. Video is now newly included in Yahoo! Groups, but can be a bit cumbersome to use. It might help to use Yahoo! Messenger alongside the group if the video option within the chat room proves difficult. So, after creating such an all-powerful environment, what to do with it?

WORKING IN AN ON-LINE LEARNING ENVIRONMENT: A CASE STUDY

An English and a French school have developed pen pal schemes over the past few years, and have recently begun to encourage pupils to exchange e-mails rather than letters, to enable a more immediate exchange and help pupils develop their computer skills. This year, two Year 9 classes have decided they would like to take the exchange further. To this end, both schools looked at their timetable and found a way to allow the two classes to communicate in real time to work on an introduction to teenage life in each country, including attitudes towards issues such as school, clothes, rules at home and pocket money. One hour a week for one term was timetabled to introduce the pupils to the technology and after this, pupils were allowed access to the computer room at lunch and after school to continue with the exchange – they may also have worked from home. The pupils decided to work with a combination of e-mails, a notice board, and audio communication in the form of a chatroom. E-mail messages are used for social communication and discussion of logistical issues, whereas the noticeboard is used for the exchange of opinions on a topic focus set by the teacher. The topic focus changes on a regular basis, covering the different aspects of teenage life. During the lesson, most of the pupils start by typing in or uploading e-mails to their partners and reading the replies they have received, taking notes of phrases and vocabulary as they go along. Once they have dealt with their own and their partners' new information, they access the Yahoo! Group where their teachers have set up the notice board with an opinion poll, asking each pupil's opinion about the current topic – e.g. what they think of their school day, how much pocket money they get, whether they think trendy clothes important, etc. This topic changes on a monthly basis. Pupils read each other's notices and reply to those that stimulate them, choosing the language depending on the complexity of the message they would like to get across. Each pupil collates 'opinion' vocabulary in a specific note book, which is checked by their teacher on a monthly basis. While the book was started in a classroom lesson compiling vocabulary the pupils anticipated they might need, additions are now based on real-life experience and exchanges prompted by their work within the bilingual group.

While other pupils are working with this written format, following their personal e-mail communication and accessing the opinion poll on the noticeboard, six pupils from each school take turns to have access to the group's chat room, rotating weekly. Here, they discuss what is happening on the notice board, exploring each other's opinions orally, typing in translations and spellings to clarify. Both teachers are logged into the chat room and make themselves available when needed – foreign language assistants and sixth formers might also help. When they are in the chat room, the teachers use the time to encourage more reluctant speakers.

If the technical set-up allows, there is nothing to stop other pupils from using Yahoo! Messenger to talk to their own partners on a one-to-one basis, as long as they do not try to access the chat room, disturbing the balance of discussion there.

After each poll finishes, pupils from each school form groups, and use their phrases and vocabulary to prepare a presentation in a format of their choice, such as PowerPoint. The presentation is vetted by the partner group. It is then placed as a file in the Yahoo! Group, accessible to all learners within the group to help them develop their ideas on exam topics, for example, or for personal interest.

As the Yahoo! Group is accessible by invitation only, pupils who wish to do so can always continue to use the facilities from home, and parents can be reassured that their child will talk only to people who have been invited to the group, either from their own class or from the French partner class.

6 Conclusion

The possibilities for communication on-line in a foreign language increase continually. From a starting point of simple written e-mails to the use of attachments, notice boards and finally real-time communication in written, oral and visual format, the question arises – what will the future bring? There are, of course, technical problems, but these will be resolved gradually as technology develops, and they are worth overcoming because of the extraordinary power on-line communication has in bringing the target language and culture into the classroom and enable contact with native speakers which might not otherwise be possible.

However, as on-line learning environments, usually called MLEs (Managed learning environment) or VLEs (Virtual learning environment), develop and become more common in schools, there are increasing opportunities for easy and secure communication with native and other speakers of the target language. On-line learning environments nearly always include most, if not all, of the communicative facilities discussed in this book. Electronic communication between teacher/tutor and pupil and also between groups of pupils working collaboratively is being used increasingly to support learning focused on electronic resources (either Web- or CD-ROM-based). Communicative facilities available via an MLE or VLE could then be extended to pupils outside the school with minimal issues of security and logistics, enabling the types of exchange with native speakers highlighted here.

There are already many collaborative projects on-line, such as the European Schoolnet (**www.eun.org**) which offers teachers and pupils a chance to find similarly minded classes and individuals to share resources with. The site also offers information and news about grants and projects and invites teachers to develop new contacts, either for themselves or for their pupils. One of its most useful features in this context, however, is the partner-finding facility – currently one of the safest opportunities for teachers to gain access to like-minded classes for an on-line exchange.

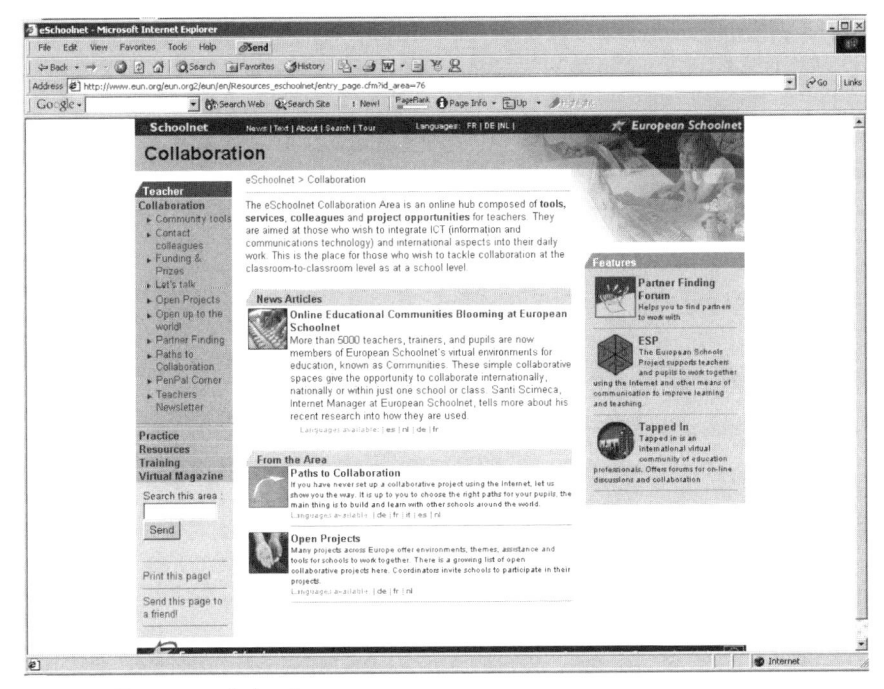

Source: European Schoolnet

On the commercial market, companies such as Digitalbrain (**www.digitalbrain.com**) and Schoolzone (**www.schoolzmail.com**) offer the set-up and management of an on-line learning community, creating a safe environment for pupils to work in, allowing for discussions and chat. They also facilitate access to the international ePALS Classroom Exchange™ (**www.epals.com**), allowing pupils to collaborate on-line. These on-line learning groups, frequently termed MLEs or VLEs, are offered by several commercial programmes, such as Blackboard (**www.blackboard.com**) and WebCT (**www.webct.com**), who specialise in customised VLEs.

Conclusion

With so many resources and organisations to choose from, it can be difficult to keep up-to-date with developments. A printed book can only give an overview of how on-line communication can work and a snapshot of what is available at any one point in time. To accommodate this, a Web page has been created at **www.cilt.org.uk/publications/communicatingonline** to accompany this book, giving live links to the websites mentioned.

List of websites

Blackboard: www.blackboard.com

British Council: Windows on the World: www.wotw.org.uk

CILT: www.cilt.org.uk
InfoTech 7: *Communicating on-line* Web page: www.cilt.org.uk/publications/communicatingonline

Department for Education and Skills: Superhighway Safety: http://safety.ngfl.gov.uk

Digitalbrain: www.digitalbrain.com

eTandem: tandem@slf3.ruhr-uni-bochum.de

European School Network: www.eun.org

European Union Safer Internet Action Plan: www.besafeonline.org

ICQ: http://web.icq.com

iVisit: www.ivisit.com

Microsoft MSN: http://messenger.msn.co.uk

Microsoft Netmeeting: www.microsft.com/windows/netmeeting

mIRC: www.mirc.com

MUDs/Moos: www.well.ac.uk/wellclas/moo/moo.htm
www.alladin.ac.uk/support/moo/about.html

PalTalk: www.paltalk.com

List of websites

ePALS Classroom Exchange™: www.epals.com
Schoolzone: www.schoolzmail.com
WebCT: www.webct.com
Yahoo!: www.yahoo.fr
Yahoo! Groups: http://groups.yahoo.com
Yahoo! Messenger: http://messenger.yahoo.com